RAILS AROUND CORK AND KERRY

An Irish Railway Pictorial

Michael H. C. Baker

Ian Allan
PUBLISHING

Front cover, top: **Cork, Glanmire Road station on 22 September 1953 with green-liveried 'B2' (GSR '400') class 4-6-0 No 407 on the 11.25 to Kingsbridge.** Neil Sprinks

Front cover, bottom: **The invention of a French engineer, Henry Lartigue, the Listowel & Ballybunion monorail opened between its namesake towns in County Kerry in 1888 with three Leeds-built Hunslet 0-3-0s as motive power. The crew on No 3 pose for the camera at Ballybunion probably around the time of the line's demise in 1924.** Author's collection

Back cover: **On 28 July 1951, 2-6-0Ts Nos 1T and 2T struggle up the 1 in 29 gradient out of Lispole on the Tralee & Dingle line. Passenger sevices over the line ceased in 1939, but monthly cattle trains operated on market days until final closure on 1 July 1953.** W. A. Aspell

Title page: **Killarney station in August 2005 as '200' class No 215 reverses out of the station with the 08.30 Dublin–Tralee service. It is backing into the headshunt and will then take the line to the left over which it is passing, climbing behind the town on its way into County Kerry and its destination. The train and notices are different but the scene has not changed over the last 50 years.** Author

First published 2005

ISBN (10) 0 7110 3158 4
ISBN (13) 978 0 7110 3158 6

Published by Ian Allan Publishing

an imprint of Ian Allan Publishing Ltd, Hersham, Surrey KT12 4RG.
Printed in England by Ian Allan Printing Ltd, Hersham, Surrey KT12 4RG.

Code: 0510/B

Visit the Ian Allan Publishing website at
www.ianallanpublishing.com

CONTENTS

Dedication

For my good friend Michael Murphy of Cobh and Cork City.

INTRODUCTION

There are few more spectacular and unspoilt coastlines in all of Europe than the west of Ireland, and Counties Cork and Kerry, down in the far south, can claim to own some of the very best. The advent of the railway promised to put such wonderful scenery within reach of the discerning traveller. However, discerning – and by necessity relatively affluent – travellers were thin on the ground throughout the great days of railway building in the second half of the 19th century. Therefore, before railway construction could become economic, there needed to be traffic flows in the opposite direction, from Cork and Kerry eastwards, which in essence meant to Dublin. Cork was the principal city of the south-west and the linking of it with the capital was one of the first objectives of the rail-builders. The terrible famine in the 1840s dealt a severe blow to the economy of Ireland, the population declining as a result of death and emigration by some eight million to six and a half million in just three years. Nevertheless in the midst of this misery the railway from Dublin to Cork opened on Monday 29 October 1849.

There was nowhere comparable in County Kerry, not in size, not in industrial capacity, not in importance as a port. But there was Killarney, which, to quote Frank O'Connor, 'the Romantic movement turned into a sort of tourist resort'. On 15 July 1853 the line from Mallow, on the Dublin to Cork route, reached Killarney. Not that this impressed O'Connor. He wrote that the town was 'a depressing hole, too wealthy for its lack of taste, and infested by hotel-keepers, touts, jarveys and boatmen, all with a glib flow of patter which also probably goes back to the Romantic movement'. O'Connor admits that the surrounding area is 'remarkable for its scenery', but then delivers as the killer blow: '. . . when you can see it, which, owing to the appalling weather the county enjoys, is very rarely'. Frank O'Connor was just about as good a writer as you could get, but he was a Cork man and traditionally the people of Cork have been somewhat scathing of those from Kerry and vice versa. Mind you, he could be pretty dismissive of his home town. 'It would be difficult for the average person over eighteen to be happy in Cork.' O'Connor once had a job as a clerk on the Great Southern & Western Railway (GS&WR) at Glanmire Road station and hated it, so perhaps we need not accept his views on railway matters without question.

Whatever O'Connor's opinion of Killarney, others took a very different view and the railway built a very fine hotel on 40 acres of land acquired, not without some reluctance, from Lord Kenmare. Known as the Great Southern, it was the first railway-owned hotel anywhere in Ireland or Britain. It was designed in the classical style by the well-known Dublin architect Frederick Darley, and did much to boost tourism. No longer railway-owned, it remains a most impressive feature of a town devoted to encouraging tourism on a grand scale.

Acknowledgements

I am particularly grateful to Neil Sprinks for allowing me to select from his wonderful collection of photographs taken when steam reigned (almost) supreme at the end of the 1940s and early 1950s, to John Langford for access to his extensive photographic collection, to Tim Moriarty, Librarian of the Irish Railway Record Society, Charles Meredith of the Railway Preservation Society of Ireland (just one of the many hats he wears) and much involved in the restoration of the GSWR Royal Saloon, Richard Casserley, custodian of his father's (and his own) priceless collection of photographs, Greg Ryan, Heritage Officer of Iarnrod Eireann, and to my wife, Maeve, for her long-suffering tolerance (but then she does bear the name of Ireland's finest steam locomotive). However, as always, any errors are mine and mine alone.

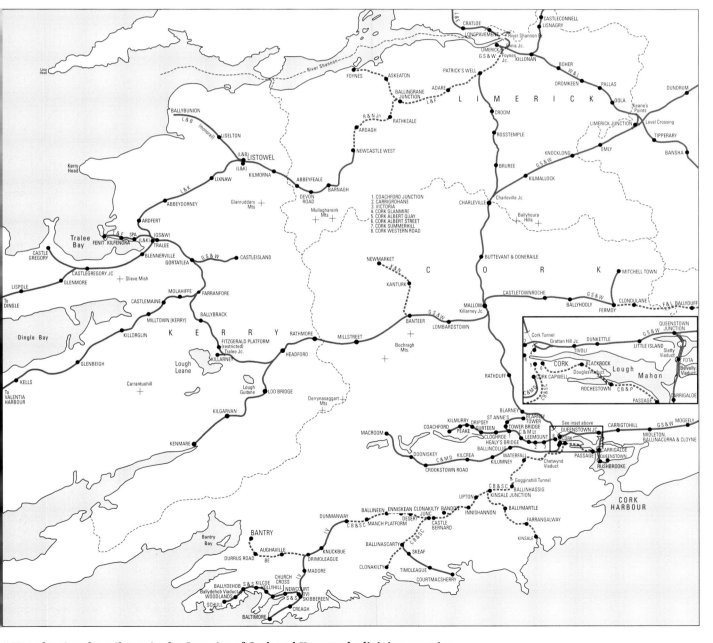

A Map showing the railways in the Counties of Cork and Kerry and adjoining counties.

CORK

Cork suffered mixed fortunes throughout the 19th century. The advent of the railway gave a boost to the cattle trade, exports increasing to England and Wales, both by way of the GS&WR and Dublin and by steamship direct from Cork, although the provision trade, once so important to the city, was in decline by the time the railway arrived and did not revive. Heavy industry, iron and steel and shipbuilding, had provided a good deal of employment, but the Famine hit this, as did competition from England, Wales and Scotland. Brewing and distilling also suffered, although these industries saw a slow revival in the second half of the 19th century. The largest flow of traffic out of Cork, and quite the saddest, was that of emigrants. In the six years between 1845 and 1851 more than one and a half million men, women and children left Ireland, and in all between 1848 and 1950 the number was six million. Of these, no fewer than two and a half million sailed from Queenstown, or Cobh as it would become, 11 miles south of Cork City. Almost all of that two and a half million would have travelled by train. For the great majority they would never return, nor see again those they had left behind. The songs, poems and stories recounting the misery, distress and anguish of these partings are legion, almost impossible to calculate. Queenstown was actually known as Cove, which is how it is pronounced today, until its renaming after a visit from Queen Victoria in 1849.

One man who left his native city as a young man to find not fortune but his vocation as a priest in England, like so many others, is my friend Michael Murphy. As a boy he lived in Cobh high up above the harbour. He recalls his father telling the story of how one May evening in 1915, shaving with a cut throat razor in front of the mirror, he suddenly stopped and called out: 'Something's going on in the harbour,' the reflection of which he could see through the bathroom window behind him. It was a flotilla of small boats dashing out to the Old Head of Kinsale in a forlorn attempt to rescue the victims of the torpedoed Cunard liner, *Lusitania*.

Then, as now, there was an intensive service on the railway line connecting Queenstown with Cork city. Let Michael Murphy conjure up the excitement of the journey in steam days:

'Was it the noise of clanging metal, the whoosh of the rushing steam, or the whistle blow of the engine that triggered the high excitement known only to travellers by train, especially if they are children? Perhaps it is some combination of all three that sends a tingle down my spine every time I enter a railway station since I first entered Cobh (Queenstown) station to board a train at the age of seven in 1933. I was heading for Cork, with my mother, to have my eyes examined by a specialist optician.

'It was on that 14-mile journey that I first experienced the thrill of the two bridges, which I said were 'the bridges going up and down'. This was my perception of movement as the train sped across those bridges, with their sides of three half hoops, which led to and from the Fota estate, with its own little station. Indeed, all the stations on the Cobh to Cork line were little stations, and had little gardens splendidly kept. Those well-kept gardens, and the obvious pride and joy in their work showed by the rail staff of those days, gave the traveller by train a sense of being valued and a feeling of security. One knew that one was in safe hands, attended to by people who knew what railways were all about. Theirs was a vocation as much as it was a job.

'On arrival at Cork's Glanmire Road (now Kent) station, after seeing the wonders of the ever-changing scene from the carriage window, I was simply overwhelmed by the sights and sounds of it all. There, close by in the train shed, were the mighty engines that pulled the trains, passenger or goods, on the main lines from Cork to Dublin, or to Kerry, or to Waterford, or to Limerick. They were being cleaned and polished and repaired, while around them little engines were shunting wagons and carriages about with great glee, just like Thomas the Tank Engine of more recent days. All this against a backdrop of ships' masts and enormous grain silos on the quay outside the station. I was to come to know that station very well in the years to come, for a year later, on 13 June 1934, we moved to Cork city, and most of the family did so by train; my Dad and my older brother, Philip, had gone in the truck that had taken our furniture.

'In our family "the station" has always, naturally, been the train station. It seemed absurd to call a bus terminus a station! I suppose that expressed our own pride in and love of trains. The train from Cork station has taken me on holidays, to sports events, to events in the life of our extended family, and to the mail boat from Dun Laoghaire to Holyhead, and on across Wales to seminary life in Warwickshire, and on again to life as a priest in the diocese of Plymouth in England.'

The year 1849 may have been the date when the first railway, from Dublin, reached Cork, but it went only as far as Blackpool in the suburbs; it would be another six years before the long tunnel into the city centre was opened for traffic. In the meantime the Cork, Blackrock & Passage company, running along the shores of Cork Harbour, had commenced operating trains on 8 June 1850 and could therefore claim to be the first to provide a service to and from the city centre. It was closely followed by the Cork & Bandon Railway, which got as far as Ballinhassig, some 10 miles from the city centre, in 1849, and reached its Albert Quay terminus, on the south bank of the Lee, in December 1851.

Next came the Cork & Youghal Railway, which had a terminus at Summerhill, directly above the mouth of the tunnel from which the Great Southern & Western trains emerged to enter their Penrose Quay station. Summerhill opened for business in October 1860, but until improvements had been completed by December 1861 trains entering and leaving it had to be horse-drawn.

The Cork & Macroom started operations in 1866 and for a while shared the Cork & Bandon's Albert Quay terminus, but the two parties fell out, as railway partners so often did, so in 1879 it took itself off to its own terminus at Capwell, the best part of a mile to the south.

The terminus of the Cork & Muskerry Railway was built on what was strictly speaking an island at Western Road, in 1887. The Cork & Muskerry was a light railway, of 3ft gauge, with lines to three destinations, Blarney, Donoughmore and Coachford.

That completes the list of railways, although not the termini, serving Cork city, but for the sake of completeness we should mention the city's tram lines. A 5ft 3in horse tramway ran between 1872 and 1875, connecting the Great Southern & Western, the Cork & Bandon, and the Cork, Blackrock & Passage stations. Much more successful were the electric trams. Operated by the Cork Electric Tramway & Lighting Company, they ran between 1898 and 1931. The gauge was 2ft 11½ in, chosen to allow narrow-gauge railway trains to share the tracks, but this never seems to have happened.

LOCOMOTIVES, STOCK AND SERVICES

Right: **No 19 was a 2-2-2 passenger engine built by Sharp Brothers for the GS&WR in 1848 for the opening of the line, and was used to haul trains between Cork and Dublin. It is of a design much favoured in Britain and Ireland in the early days of railways and the GS&WR had 20 of them. The class was withdrawn in the 1870s.**
Ian Allan Library (IAL)

Right: **There were also 20 2-2-2s built by Bury, Curtis & Kennedy, which were similar in some respects, although they differed in having bar frames and tall, dome-shaped firebox casings. E. L. Ahrons in his *Locomotive and Train Working in the Latter Part of the Nineteenth Century*, originally published in the *Railway Magazine* in 1925, remarks that 'the locomotives had to be, and were, a very game lot, to rattle over such a road without being shaken to pieces en route. Not only did they manage to hold together, but some of the old Sharp's and Bury's engines covered a very big mileage during the course of their existence.' One, No 36, somehow managed to survive beyond that date, and today can be seen, wearing a slightly neglected air in the somewhat neglected concourse of Cork's Kent (formerly Glanmire Road) station.**
Rev Michael Murphy

Penrose Quay, the terminus of the line from Dublin, lasted until 1893. In 1866 the Great Southern & Western Railway (GS&WR) acquired the Cork & Youghal Railway, but it was not until 1890 that the former decided to combine its own station with that of the latter, and in 1893 the present station, the only one surviving in Cork city, was opened at Glanmire Road (in 1966 its name was changed to Kent [Ceannt] in commemoration of one of the leading members of the 1916 Easter).

Heading west, in 1863 the Cork & Bandon Railway opened a branch 10¾ miles long from Kinsale Junction, west of Ballinhassig, to the fishing port and naval base at Kinsale. A change of name to the Cork, Bandon & South Coast Railway came about in 1888, by which time it worked lines to Clonakilty, Courtmacsherry and Skibbereen on the south coast, and Bantry on an inlet to the west. In 1893 the Skibbereen branch was extended to Baltimore. In 1893 the Cork, Bandon & South Coast Railway possessed a route mileage of 94 miles.

A 3ft narrow-gauge railway, the Schull & Skibbereen Light Railway, was opened on 9 September 1886, and ran along the roadside and past the splendidly named Roaring Water Bay to Ballydehob and Schull.

Inevitably with the spread of the motor car, bus and lorry to the most remote areas of the west in the 1920s, the railway began to lose out, first its passenger and then its freight traffic, to the roads. The Fermoy to Mitchelstown branch, east of Mallow, closed completely on 1 December 1953, while the main line through Fermoy, from Waterford to Mallow, ceased operations on 27 March 1967. Regular trains ceased on the Youghal branch on 2 June 1978, although beet traffic lasted until 1981 and passenger specials continued until 1988. However, the track remained in place and services are due to restart as far as Midleton. The Cork Albert Street to Monkstown service ended on 12 September 1932, the section beyond Monkstown to Crosshaven having gone on 1 June that year, while the Cork to Coachford, Donoughmore and Blarney lines closed on 31

December 1934. The Macroom line ceased on 1 December 1953.

In West Cork the Kinsale branch was closed on 1 September 1931. In the far west the Schull & Skibbereen ceased operations on 27 January 1947. In one fell swoop all the remaining railway operations in West Cork, the Clonakilty, Courtmacsherry and Baltimore branches, and the main line to Bantry, ceased on 1 April 1961. All that was left was the connection across Cork City to Albert Quay, and goods services continued to operate here until 12 April 1976.

It was inevitable that the lines in rural Cork would succumb to the road motor vehicle for their chief business was serving the needs of agriculture and the people who worked the land. The lorry and the bus could reach parts of the county distant from the railway and offered a more flexible service. Tourism, chiefly from England and more often than not Cork natives or their descendants returning for a visit to the old home, was a factor and although the train often had the advantage here, being more comfortable and better able

Left: **At the other extreme were the three magnificent 'B1a' class 4-6-0s built in 1939-40, and this is the view from the cab of No 800** Maedhbh **and she speeds north-east with a Cork to Dublin express in about 1948. Restricted by their weight and length to the Dublin to Cork main line, World War 2, subsequent fuel restrictions and then dieselisation scarcely gave them a chance to show their paces, but there is little doubt that they were the equal of the 'Kings', 'Castles' and rebuilt 'Royal Scots'.**
National Railway Museum, York

Below left: **No 263, one of the powerful eight-strong 'J4' class of 0-6-0s, designed by R. E. L. Maunsell in 1913 before his move to Ashford as Chief Mecanical Engineer of the South Eastern & Chatham Railway (SECR), heads into Waterford with a goods from Cork in September 1959.** Author

Above right: **The boat trains that ran between Rosslare, Waterford, Mallow and Cork were often hauled from the 1920s onwards by another class of Maunsell engines, the Woolwich 2-6-0s. These were to a design of the SECR that was taken up by the War Department after World War 1, which had a number built at Woolwich Arsenal to try and provide continuing employment for munitions workers after the war. Unwanted by most of the English main line companies, the parts were sold off cheaply, 26 being assembled in Ireland, and all being in service with the GSR by 1925. They proved an excellent investment. In this picture No 398 is in charge of a Cork to Dublin express; the second carriage is a former Pullman Car, one of four put into service in 1926.** IAL

to carry luggage, the holiday season was relatively short. Moreover, once the shipping companies introduced vehicle ferries after World War 2, not even the attractions of panoramic views from comfortable diesel railcars, which were introduced on the West Cork lines in 1954, could compete with the motor coach and the private car.

The Cork, Bandon & South Coast Railway owned 20 locomotives (somehow one expected there to be rather more) at the time of its absorption into the Great Southern Railway (GSR) in November 1924. These consisted of two 4-4-2Ts, which had started out as Neilson 4-4-0Ts in 1894 and were rebuilt in 1898/1900, another, built by Dübs in 1891 and rebuilt as a 4-4-2T in1902, one home-built 4-4-0T of 1901, two Dübs 2-4-0Ts of 1874/75, five Beyer Peacock 0-6-0STs of 1881/82/87/90/94, whilst the remaining nine were all 4-6-0Ts. One of these, built by Dübs in 1891, had begun as a 4-4-0T before being

rebuilt in 1906. The rest, built by Beyer Peacock, entered service between 1906 and 1920 and were the mainstay of both passenger and goods services until the end of steam. The wheel arrangement may have been unusual but these were excellent engines. Classified 'B4' by the GSR, examples even migrated to Dublin, where they were much appreciated on suburban services out of Amiens Street and Harcourt Street, but they will for ever be associated with their native heath of West Cork. Two even outlived the closure of the West Cork lines, not being withdrawn until 1963. There is little point in wishing for the moon but one would have loved to have seen one of these characterful locomotives preserved. The best we can do is a handsome and very accurate mural of one which graces a wall in Skibbereen.

The Cork to Passage line was standard 5ft 3in gauge for the first 50 years of its existence, from 1850 to 1900, and was worked by three Sharp Bros 2-2-2 well tanks. When converted to 3ft gauge at the opening of the 20th century, four 2-4-2Ts were bought from Neilson Reid. They looked rather like an adaptation, certainly from the running plate upwards, of a standard gauge design, with cousins across the water in Lancashire and Yorkshire, and were speedy, powerful machines. All were transferred in 1933 to the Cavan and Leitrim section when their own line closed. One was scrapped in 1936 but the other three went on for a considerable time longer, two lasting until this line closed in 1959.

The Cork & Macroom Direct Railway (C&MDR) owned one Andrew Barclay locomotive, an 0-6-2T of 1904, much its most modern and powerful acquisition, four 2-4-0Ts built by Dübs between 1865 and 1881, and a 2-4-2T which had originated on the Waterford, Limerick & Western Railway in 1891, and was bought from the Great Southern & Western in 1914. None of this assortment survived the

C&MDR's closure in 1935, all being scrapped before the year was out.

The Cork & Muskerry Light Railway handed seven locomotives on to the GSR. Unlike the companies we have so far considered, these all gloried in names. Two were 0-4-4Ts built by T. Green (not exactly a household name) in 1892/3, the rest 4-4-0Ts, three by Falcon, dating from 1887 and 1898, one by Brush built in 1904, and one by Hunslet, built as late as 1919. The Hunslet, GSR No 4K *Blarney*, despite coming from a manufacturer much favoured by narrow gauge lines, lasted a mere eight years, an extraordinary state of affairs, whilst one from the obscure Green works, No 6K *The Muskerry*, was the only one considered fit for further service after the Cork & Muskerry closed in 1934, being transferred westwards to the Schull & Skibbereen where it lasted until 1954, outliving all the other Cork & Muskerry motive power by at least 19 years.

The Schull & Skibbereen Tramway and Light Railway (West Carberry Tramways and Light Railways) owned just about sufficient engines to do justice to the length of the name of the company. A Dick Kerr 0-4-0T of 1886, a Nasmyth Wilson 4-4-0T of 1888 and two Peckett 4-4-0Ts of 1906 and 1914 passed to the GSR. Running as it did for most of its length alongside roads, it was a sitting duck for motor competition. Trains ceased during the fuel crisis of 1947 and never ran again although several of the engines lingered on, rusting away until broken up in 1954.

The main line of the Great Southern & Western, Ireland's principal railway company (although the Great Northern would not have agreed), the 165-mile route from Dublin to Cork, has always been provided with the most up-to-date motive power. Although without any severe gradients for nearly all its length, a few sections are taxing in the extreme. Out of Heuston (Kingsbridge) there is a mile and a half at 1 in 117, then a section as far as

Inchicore at 1 in 84, easing to 1 in 138 until milepost 4¼ is reached. But this is as nothing compared to the gradients encountered by trains attempting to get away from Cork. The three-quarter-mile-long tunnel at the start is at 1 in 78-64, then follow two miles at 1 in 60, and although the gradient then eases the climb continues until milepost 14 is reached. Almost all trains in steam days were double-headed out of Cork, whilst triple-heading was not uncommon.

2-2-2s were the order of the day in the beginning for passenger traffic, with 0-4-2s used for freight. It is remarkable that one of the original Bury single drivers, No 36, dating from 1847, has managed to survive. One of a class of 14, it remained at work until 1875, covering 360,000 miles in that time, and today can be seen in the entrance to Kent station, Cork. Having initially imported locomotives from England, the GS&WR began building its own at Inchicore in 1852, turning out 2-2-2s, 0-4-2s and 0-6-0s. In 1864 Alexander MacDonnell, a graduate of Trinity College, Dublin, was appointed locomotive engineer, and with him we enter the modern era for his designs could still be seen at work almost one hundred years later. Indeed an example of his most numerous class, the '101s', more commonly known as the 'J15' class 0-6-0, is still out and about on the Irish railway network as I write. A total of 119 'J15' were built between 1867 and 1903 and they lasted, often rebuilt but still the same essential maids of all work, until the end of steam. McDonnell introduced the 4-4-0 to Ireland and numerous variations were produced down the years, being very familiar in and around Cork. The last five were 'D4s' (GSR Class 342'), with Great Western Railway-style outside frame bogies, constructed at Inchicore in 1936 and used on the Cork to Rosslare boat trains.

The 4-6-0 arrived in 1905/7 in the shape of six Robert Coey goods engines of the GSR

Left: **No 409 heads the up Mail near Kilbarry around 1928 – a ballast train is passing on the down line. The carriages, with the exception of the clerestory attached to the mail van, are just about the most up-to-date, as one would expect of such a prestigious train. Built in 1922 but not put into service because of Civil War problems until 1923, No 409 was taken out of service and scrapped in 1930. That this express passenger engine, introduced with such high hopes, should have lasted a mere seven years at a time of almost unparalleled financial stringency, speaks volumes about its inadequacy.** Rex Murphy

Class 362 class. They worked heavy freights on the main line with only limited success, being prone to derailments, and all were broken up by 1930. More successful were four 2-6-0s, Nos 368-71. Much the best known and popular of this wheel arrangement were 26 'K1' and 'K1a' locomotives. These were designed by R. E. L. Maunsell, who was in charge at Inchicore between 1911 and 1913, from where he moved to Ashford to become Chief Mechanical Engineer (CME) of the South Eastern & Chatham Railway (SECR) and then, in 1923, the Southern Railway. However, none of these engines came out during Maunsell's reign in Dublin, his one new design in that period being a 4-4-0, *William Goulding*. By all accounts this very large locomotive did excellent work on the Cork Mails but it is weight upset the civil engineers department and its life was a short one. The Maunsell 2-6-0s were an SECR design, taken up by the War Department and built at Woolwich. They appeared too late for war service and eventually the Midland Great Western Railway bought 12 in the form of a kit of parts, to which the Great Southern added another 15, although only 26 engines actually appeared. Although they became the principal passenger engines on the Midland main line they were familiar in Cork, indeed my last sight of one was in Cork shed in 1961, their penultimate year in service. None of the Irish examples have been preserved but several of the very similar former Southern Railway ones remain.

Finally came the passenger 4-6-0s. E. A. Watson arrived at Inchicore in 1913 with an excellent pedigree, having previously held positions of responsibility with the Pennsylvania Railroad, and the Great Western Railway, each claiming, with some justification, to be the best on opposite sides of the Atlantic. Sadly Watson's 10 big, four-cylinder 'B2' class 4-6-0s, were a disappointment. Within a few years three were scrapped and the rest heavily rebuilt as two-cylinder engines, after which they performed satisfactorily, between Dublin and Cork. Watson's successor, J. R. Bazin, brought out

Above: **No 407 passing Rathpeacon at the summit of the 3-mile-long 1 in 60 climb from Glanmire Road station, Cork, with the Up Mail. The locomotive's designer E. A. Watson had been Assistant Works Manager at Swindon, and his big four-cylinder 4-6-0s, quite the largest locomotives in the country, showed the influence of Churchward's 'Stars', as well as giving a nod to the London & North Western Railway's 'Claughtons'. The first came out in 1916; No 407 was built by Armstrong Whitworth and delivered in October 1922. For some extraordinary reason it had a saturated boiler, and in its first few months of service it was burning 26% more coal than its superheated brothers, so as quickly as possible, in May 1925 to be precise, it was fitted with a superheated boiler. Unfortunately this** merely turned a very bad engine into a fairly bad one. Falling far short of the magnificent 'Stars', nor as good as the erratic 'Claughtons', the '400s' were a disaster. Despite the parlous financial state of the Great Southern in the early years of Eire's independence, four of the ten had been scrapped by 1930 and the others converted, at considerable expense, to two-cylinder machines. In this splendid Rex Murphy picture, taken around 1929, No 407 is seen in original condition, a fine-looking engine but, oh, how looks can deceive! She was the last of her class to be converted, in 1938, having 'lingered on with four cylinders as spare engine in Cork, hardly ever in steam,' to quote R. N. Clements. In two-cylinder form No 407 lasted until replaced by diesels in 1955. Rex Murphy

Right: **This picture has been reproduced before, but it can bear another outing for it marks a significant occasion. Six trilby hats are seen together in front of No 800 *Maedhbh*, the date is 2 October 1950, and Ireland's most famous steam engine has just arrived at Cork with the inaugural 'Enterprise' from Belfast via Dublin. This train covered 278 miles, quite the longest regular through run in the country, although, of course, engines were changed in Dublin. Although the 'Enterprise' only served Cork for three years, it attracted sufficient attention to appear on the cover of the *Meccano Magazine*. The 'Enterprise' name survives on the Dublin to Belfast route to this day.**
Walter McGrath collection

three 'B1' class 4-6-0s, Nos 500-2, which were intended as mixed traffic engines, but they proved to be perfectly capable of working the principal passenger trains between Cork and Dublin. The 1930s was a period of severe economic hardship in Eire and the Great Southern Railway was able to build very few new locomotives. However, with the introduction of modern carriages for the principal Cork to Dublin expresses, it was felt that a new class of 4-6-0 was justified. The result was quite the finest steam locomotives ever to run in Ireland.

A. W. Harty was CME from 1932 to 1937 at the GSR, E. C. Bredin succeeding him, but it was J. J. Johnston, later Assistant CME, and the team of draughtsmen and engineers at Inchicore, who were largely responsible for No 800. Completed in April 1939 after several weeks of trials in which various minor modifications and adjustments were made, the big 4-6-0 was brought back into Inchicore at the end of June. She emerged, not in the standard, utilitarian grey but in a light blue-green, picked out with black and yellow lining. The finishing touch was her name. The 26 counties had finally wrested their independence from Britain some 17 years earlier and No 800 bore brass letters on a blue background spelling out in Gaelic script 'Maedhbh' ('Maeve)', the name of the legendary pre-Christian queen of Ireland. The question was, would she be as good as she looked? Bearing in mind the disappointment of her '400' class predecessors, this was by no means a foregone conclusion.

On 17 July 1939 she made her inaugural run on the down Cork Mail. Mark Foley was her driver and Mat Ryan her fireman, both Inchicore men. Hauling the regular load of 300 tons she was ahead of schedule at practically every stop and emerged triumphantly from the tunnel into Glanmire Road station, Cork, five minutes early. A celebration dinner, presided over by Bredin, was held at the Great Southern Hotel, and then, with a Cork crew of driver Broderick and fireman Sheehan in charge, she returned

to Dublin. Throughout that summer *Maedhbh* performed in a way never seen before in Ireland. It was not fanciful to claim that her achievements were as big an advance over her predecessors as were those of Gresley's and Stanier's streamliners over what had gone before on their respective lines. O. S. Nock was on her footplate one August day when *Maedhbh* was in charge of no less than 450 tons, with passengers from a liner which had called at Cobh and a great many holidaymakers. Remarkably, the authorities decided to provide no assistance on the climb through the dripping wet Glanmire Road tunnel. Nock describes it as the stiffest job he had ever seen asked of a 4-6-0 but *Maedhbh* was equal to it and with 50% cut off and almost full regulator she blasted up the bank at a steady 23mph. Not only was she immensely strong but she was economical, a vital attribute, and fast, probably capable of exceeding 100mph — 96mph near Thurles was the highest recorded speed she attained.

Later that year *Maedhbh* was joined by her sister, No 801 *Macha*, and the two took charge of the Cork Mails. The schedule was cut and this was maintained throughout 1940, the Irish Free State being, initially, unaffected by the outbreak of war. In June that year, the third of the sisters, No 802 *Tailte* came out of Inchicore, allowing *Maedhbh* to retire there, temporarily, for overhaul. By the following summer the brief, glorious heyday of the three 'Queens' was over. Coal supplies became so severely restricted that by 1943 there was only one passenger/mail train each way between Dublin and Cork. It took a long time for schedules to return to pre-war standards and, by the time they did, diesel railcars, introduced in 1952, were operating them, to be succeeded by the 'A' class diesel-electric locomotives three years later. Boiler pressures on the '800s' were reduced and Nos 801/2

were rebuilt with single blast pipes. Their weight and size restricted them to the Cork to Dublin main line, where there was now little work for them. No.802 *Tailte* was withdrawn in 1957, and although her sisters survived into the 1960s they were something of an embarrassment to the operating authorities. My only sight of one in action was *Macha*, externally immaculate, hauling a miniscule freight up the bank out of Glanmire Road, a task a 'J15' 0-6-0 would have taken in its stride. She was broken up the next year but *Maedhbh*, Ireland's largest and finest steam locomotive, was been preserved. Unlikely ever to steam again, bearing in mind her very restricted route availability, *Maedhbh* is still a splendid sight, restored to her original magnificence in the Ulster Folk & Transport Museum at Cultra on the shores of Belfast Lough.

Whilst not altogether suitable for long-distance travel, the Park Royal diesel railcars were popular with the travelling public, providing universal standards of comfort, unlike their steam-hauled counterparts where carriages might range from the very latest to arc-roofed ancients dating back some 50 years. The Metropolitan-Vickers Sulzer-engined 'A' class Co-Co diesel-electric locomotives which arrived in 1955 enabled the railcars to be gradually cascaded to Dublin suburban work and there was a speeding up of schedules, the fastest Dublin to Cork timing coming down to 3hr 28min. Not that this was always adhered to for the Sulzer engines proved to be an Achilles heel of the 'A' class locomotives and they frequently broke down. Re-engining by General Motors (GM) eventually solved the problem, by which time General Motors Bo-Bo locomotives, one-off designs developed especially for CIE, had entered service. They proved a wonderful investment, double-heading the principal and increasingly heavy

Left: **I have just said that No 409 was scrapped in 1930 – so what is it doing here some 20 years later hauling the 'Enterprise'? R. N. Clements noted that when the order went out in 1930 that Nos 404 and 408 were to be condemned, No 404 had always seemed to me to be the best and most reliable of the four-cylinder engines; apparently I was not alone in so thinking for a switch of number-plates was quietly made, and 409 was broken up in her place.' So the engine seen here is the original 404, which had taken on the identity of 409 and been rebuilt with two cylinders. It is seen emerging from the tunnel beyond Glanmire Road station, with a set of GNR carriages bound for Belfast on the 'Enterprise'. IAL**

Below left: **For a time the 9.00am Cork to Dublin non-stop express was named 'Failte'. It is seen here hauled by one of the original 950hp General Motors Bo-Bo diesel-electrics, No B129, in its as-delivered grey livery passing Limerick Junction on 31 August 1963. Although not really powerful enough for such prestigious duties, these locomotives proved a most worthwhile investment. The last examples remained in service until the 21st century. IAL**

trains on the Dublin to Cork line.

In 1976 a much more powerful 2,475hp Co-Co, the '071' class, arrived from the La Grange, Illinois, works of General Motors, and the 18 locomotives took over from their smaller brethren. The next generation to arrive was the yet more powerful '201' class, rated at 3,200hp, built, this time at the London, Ontario, works of General Motors. There are 34 of these and they enabled the last of the by now elderly re-engined 'A' class, as well as some of the early GM Bo-Bo locomotives, to be withdrawn.

CIE invested in an extensive carriage building programme in the 1950s, although, with the end of steam haulage, the somewhat retrograde step was adopted by Inchicore of building a fleet of four-wheel vans to house the steam heating apparatus as it had been decided not to add to the complications of diesel haulage by fitting this in the locomotives. The early 1960s marked the virtual end of carriage building at Inchicore, for the next stage was the purchase of 55 coaches from Cravens of Sheffield. Some

arrived complete, others were fitted out on arrival. These are presently the oldest carriages operated by Irish Rail. Heating in these is still by steam and they run attached to the last survivors of converted British Rail Mk 1 vans and 'Dutch' vans, so called because they were built at Dundalk to a Dutch design. The result is that on winter days a bygone era is often created when a Cravens set comes to rest at a station, with copious amounts of steam gushing upwards from its nether regions.

In 1972, to a great publicity flourish, the 'Super Trains' arrived. These were BREL Mk 2D air-conditioned carriages. Basically excellent vehicles, their Inchicore-designed interior appointments were disappointing and rather old fashioned. Bogie vans of similar outline accompanied them, packed with diesel generators and all the equipment necessary to provide power for lighting, heating, air-conditioning and cooking.

The late 1980s saw the arrival of the next generation of BREL carriages from Derby, 100 Mk 3s with automatic doors, which initially

gave problems for the Inchicore engineers until reliability of operation was established. The latest stock has always worked on the Dublin to Cork line although the Mk 3s are now quite elderly. The future looks like seeing the renaissance of the railcar, this time from Japan, working an hourly service between Dublin and Cork, carrying more passengers at higher speeds than ever before.

In 2005 there are seven through trains in each direction on the Dublin to Cork line, Monday to Saturday, the fastest taking two hours, 42 minutes in the down direction, stopping at Portlaoise, Thurles, Limerick Junction and Mallow. The fastest up train is the 07.00 out of Cork which, stopping only at Mallow and Limerick Junction, reaches Dublin in two hours, 33 minutes.

Kent Station, whilst historically interesting and not without architectural merit, has not kept up with the times and is in serious need of modernising. I have stood there for some time, corralled with a large crowd of other intending passengers, under cover but nevertheless exposed to blasts of ice-cold air on a miserable winter's day, waiting to be allowed on to the Dublin train, only to find when we eventually gained access that some of us had to stand for the entire journey. However, the good news is that the Chairman of CIE, Dr Lynch, announced in February 2005

Right: **The Cork to Dublin Day Mail (it actually continued to Dun Laoghaire Carlisle Pier) was just about the most heavily loaded passenger train on CIE metals and might total 13 or 14 vehicles. It is seen here in the 1970s, headed by re-engined 'A' class Co-Co No A23R, its carriages a mixture of 1950 wooden-framed, steel-sided vehicles, and 1960-vintage Cravens; the leading vehicle is a Dundalk-assembled 'Dutch Van' heating/guards-van.** Author

that 24 million Euros has been set aside to refurbish the station, whilst on 31 January 2005 the Minister for Transport, Martin Cullen, signed an order for 120 Inter-City railcars, costing 262 million Euros, to be bought from Mitsui & Co Ltd of Japan which will revolutionise travel between Cork and Dublin - and elsewhere.

The 'Cork Mail' was probably the most prestigious train in all of Ireland, carrying as it did urgent correspondence across the Atlantic, the fastest route from New York to London being via Queenstown, Kingstown and Holyhead. More than once in the 1970s I was lucky enough to travel in the cab of the locomotive hauling the 'Day Mail' on the last stage of its journey from Heuston via the Loop Line, through the heart of Dublin to Dun Laoghaire. The train consisted of some 13 or 14 vehicles, with ordinary carriages, a diner, often one of a pair of rebuilt former GSWR cars dating from World War 1, luggage and mail vans, a daunting task for a rebuilt 'A' class. The 'Cork Mail' ceased in January 1994, the very last mail carried on Irish railways was on the 19.10 Dublin Heuston to Cork on 9 May 2005.

The decline in freight is a sorry story. Cork and its docks once provided the railways with a vast amount of business of many varieties, ranging from cattle, a trade which outlived that in the UK, oil, containers and much else. But whilst in the rest of Europe there is a drive to put as much freight on rails as possible, in Ireland the Government and Irish Rail appear to be blaming each other for the fact that in the mid-1990s rail freight accounted for 16% of all transport volume whereas in 2005 this had fallen to 3%. Figures for rail freight in the 15 EU countries for the period 1991-2003 show Ireland had the largest drop in freight carryings, at 32.4%. Admittedly, Ireland is a relatively small country, surrounded by water, and freight competes best when carried long distances, across international borders, but when one considers European Union figures which show that rail is 27 times safer than road, that an average freight train can remove 40 heavy goods vehicles journeys from the roads, that rail produces 80% less carbon dioxide per tonne carried than road, and that rail freight's external costs are four times less per tonne per kilometre than road, then the situation is disappointing. (Statistics from the June 2005 edition of the *Irish Railway News*, journal of the Irish Railway Record Society.)

In February 2005 Irish Rail increased its container-carrying charges by 25% and, to quote the *Irish Railway News*, 'carrying plummeted . . . On 1 February, the 11.45 Dublin North Wall–Cork North Esk departed . . . with all 12 container-pocket-wagons empty'. One hopes it is not too late to turn things round but when one learns that with the end of container trains 'the gantries at Charleville, Mallow and Longford have been dismantled', the outlook is not hopeful. A traditional traffic, which, thankfully, still survives, is that of beet. All Irish sugar beet is now processed at Mallow and, looking to an assured future, Irish Rail in February 2005 sought tenders for 80 open-top, second-hand containers to carry the beet to Mallow on bogie containers.

Below **The GS&WR built a set of vestibuled clerestory-roof carriages for the opening of the Rosslare-Cork service in 1906. One of these, No 861, a magnificent 66-feet-long clerestory-roof Brake Composite, survived into the late 1960s, being used on the workmen's train that ran from Inchicore down to Kingsbridge (Heuston). I managed to get a ride in it, the only time I can ever recall experiencing the unique beat of a six-wheel bogie, but I feared for its future when I next saw it at Sallins, where in those days condemned stock was taken before being broken up. Fortunately at the 11th hour the Railway Preservation Society of Ireland stepped in and No 861 is now safe at their headquarters in Whitehead, although in need of a good deal of restoration.** Author

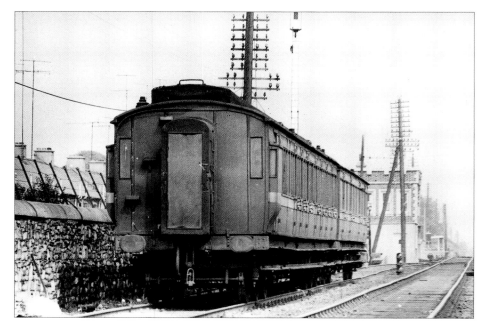

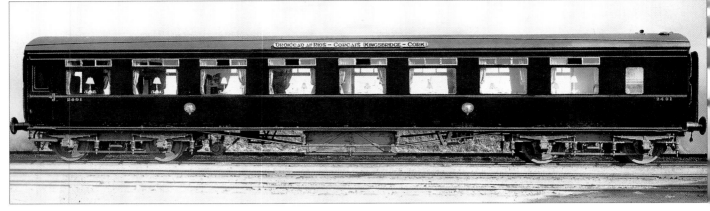

Above: **No 2401 was a dining car modernised by the Great Southern Railway in 1935 to work in the Dublin to Cork Day Mail. The cash-strapped GSR built very few new carriages, but the prestige services on its principal main line demanded the best, so steel-panelled vehicles made their appearance here in the period immediately before World War 2. The destination board is lettered in both Gaelic and English.** IAL

Below left: **Smaller, metal boards were used for a while by CIE in the early post-war years, as shown here on composite No 2125 built in 1952.** IAL

Bottom left: **A 1st Class passenger on a Dublin to Cork express in 1935. The lady is Nell Browne, the sister of perhaps the most celebrated Irish photographer of the 20th century, Father Francis Browne. Born in Cork in 1880, he joined the Jesuit Order in 1899, and while studying at the Royal University, Dublin, he found himself a classmate of James Joyce and is mentioned several times in Finnegan's Wake. As a chaplain to the Irish Guards in Flanders during World War 1, he was wounded five times and gassed once. He was awarded the Military Cross and Bar, the French Croix de Guerre and the Belgian Croix de Guerre. His** commanding officer described him as 'the bravest man I ever met'. Kodak was so impressed with his photographic abilities that they gave him free film for life. Winner of many photographic awards, Vice-President of Ireland's first Salon of Photography, this remarkable man is perhaps best know for the series of pictures he took while travelling on the *Titanic* from Southampton and Cherbourg to Queenstown, a 1st Class ticket given him by his uncle, the Bishop of Cloyne, enabling him to capture what might fairly be described as the scoop of the century! Father Francis Browne

Bottom right: **In another Father Browne picture, a passenger sits in the restaurant car of a Cork to Dublin express, reading *The Cork Examiner*, in 1933.** Father Francis Browne

Above: **Steam still visits Cork from time to time, courtesy of the Railway Preservation Society of Ireland. Former NCC 2-6-4T No 4 pilots former GNR 'S' class 4-4-0 No 171 *Slieve Gullion* as they climb away from Cork with a rail tour on 27 April 1969.**
K. Groundwater

CORK TO COBH AND
THE YOUGHAL LINE

Above right: **A train pulls out of Cork Kent, formerly Glanmire Road, for Cobh in 1996 headed by a General Motors 950hp Bo-Bo. The leading vehicle is a former British Railways Mk 1 converted to a GSV (guards steam-heating van), and the other three are Cravens, which have served CIE and IR so well.** Author's collection

Right: **No 334, a GS&WR 'D4' class 4-4-0 of 1907, speeds alongside the banks of the River Lee some time in the 1920s on its way to Cobh with what is pretty certainly, judging by both the locomotive and the relatively modern corridor carriages, a mail train from Dublin connecting with a transatlantic liner.** Author's collection

Left: **No A16, one of the original Metro-Vickers Sulzer-engined 'A' class Co-Cos of 1955, is also seen running along the waters edge near Dunkettle on its way towards Cobh in the summer of 1969 with a train consisting of a modern CIE-built four-wheel heating van and four GS&WR-built non-corridor carriages.** Author

Below: **A 'J15' 0-6-0 pulls out of Dunkettle with a train from Queenstown in about 1920.** Author's collection

Bottom: **Also at Dunkettle, on 14 September 1955, a 'J15' 0-6-0 is arriving with the 10.30am Cobh to Cork train. By this date the locomotive had been fitted with a larger boiler and Belpaire firebox, like so many but by no means all of its class.** H. C. Casserley

Above: **Re-engined Metro-Vickers Co-Co No A58R swings south towards Cobh at Cobh Junction**, as it was known when this picture was taken in August 1969; originally Queenstown Junction, it is now known as Glounthaune. To take the picture I stood on the rails of the Youghal branch, where the two tracks become one. At this date regular services over the branch had ceased, although the occasional excursion still ran (but not on that day!). Author

Right: **GM Bo-Bo No B165 enters Cobh Junction with the 17.20 Cobh to Cork service on 20 March 1975. The Youghal line can just be seen behind the train.** Aubrey Dale

Below: **This is the signalbox at Midleton on the Youghal branch. The station here, closed for many years, is due to re-open and become the terminus of a commuter service serving Mallow, Blarney and Cork.** Aubrey Dale

Top: **At Youghal, on 10 June 1932, 2-4-2T No 34 is about to depart with its train of five six-wheelers forming the 7.30pm service to Cork.** H. C. Casserley

Above: **Immediately beyond Cobh Junction, the Cobh line crosses an inlet of the harbour by way of the Belvelly Bridge. This suffered during the Civil War and one of the spans can be seen blown into the water in October 1922 . W. A. Swanton recalls that 'happily . . . there was a train at the Cobh end of the line, and this was used as far as the breached bridge, from whence we passengers then crossed the breach by a cat-walk that had been improvised for the purpose, and so connected with the 'Cork' part of the train at Fota proper.'** Walter McGrath collection

Left: **This photograph shows Queenstown station in GS&WR days, with No 59, an Aspinall Class D17 4-4-0, at the head of a train about to depart** Author

Above: **Re-engined 'A' class No 013 is seen at Cobh on 8 June 1977 with suburban train No 1017, the 14.20 service to Cork.** A. G. Merrells

Right: **Generations of immigrants sailed from Queenstown for a new and hopefully better life across the Atlantic. In the other direction, the rail link between Queenstown and Dublin, then across the Irish Sea to Holyhead and on by train to Euston, also provided the fastest service for mail and for those passengers, usually 1st Class, in a hurry to travel between New York and London. The most famous sailing of all from Queenstown was the ill-fated** *Titanic* **on 11 April 1912. The station, still served by a frequent train service from Cork, has been reduced in size and most of the original buildings now house the 'Queenstown Experience', which tells the story of its links with the New World and those who migrated from Ireland.** Author

ALBERT STREET

Above: **Back in Cork, opposite the city tram depot was Albert Street station, the terminus of the Cork, Blackrock & Passage Railway from 1873 to its closure in 1932. Originally standard gauge, it became 3ft gauge in 1900, and thereafter four Neilson 2-4-2Ts had a monopoly of the line. No 7 is seen here about to set off for Monkstown on 10 June 1932 – the section on from there to Crosshaven had closed ten days earlier. For much of its route the line ran along the southern** shore of the River Lee towards the harbour side at Crosshaven. A once very successful company, which also operated steamboats, it suffered from competition, first from the tramway and then from buses. W. A. Swanton, in his *Cork's Early Buses*, describes a hairy incident involving his brother near Monkstown, served by both railway and buses, during the Civil War. He was driving a motorcycle and sidecar, rather than a bus, 'when, rounding a corner, he came upon a trench cut in the road, and much too close for him to stop to avoid it. He must have quickly grasped the situation, for he opened the throttle and gained sufficient speed to enable the machine to jump the trench' – not something he would presumably have tried with a bus. On another occasion on a journey to Liverpool he was unable to go by train from Cork to Dublin owing to a bridge having been blown up on the main line, so his father kept him at home until '. . . to my schoolboy's delight . . . I was able to board the White Star liner *Baltic* in Cork Harbour and so to Liverpool.' H. C. Casserley

Below: **No 7 is seen again on the same day returning from Monkstown and approaching Albert Street along the only stretch of narrow-gauge double-track railway in Ireland.** H. C. Casserley

Above: **Three of the four CB&PR 2-4-2Ts pose for their photograph at Albert Street on 10 June 1932.** H. C. Casserley

Below: **The 2-4-2Ts were excellent locomotives and, despite their large (for the narrow gauge) driving wheels (4ft 6in), which enabled them to cover the 16 miles between Crosshaven and Cork non-** stop in 35 minutes, all were transferred to the Cavan & Leitrim section. **Our old friend No 7, now renumbered 13L, is seen here on a mixed train at Mohill in 1950. It was withdrawn in 1954.** Kelland Collection

ALBERT QUAY AND WEST CORK

Left: **Albert Quay station, the terminus of the standard-gauge lines serving West Cork and the principal station of the Cork, Bandon & South Coast Railway, was opened in 1851 and closed 110 years later, and was virtually next door to the Cork, Blackrock & Passage terminus at Albert Street. One of the more intriguing sights in the City of Cork was the passage of goods trains through the streets on the City Railway from Glanmire Road station across the harbour to Albert Quay; the line opened in January 1912 and closed in April 1976. No 552, an 0-6-0T built by Kitsons for the Midland Great Western Railway, heads away from Albert Quay across the River Lee on 22 September 1953.** Neil Sprinks

Centre left: **Twenty-one years later, travelling in the opposite direction, General Motors No B192 is seen with the 10.30 goods from Kent to Albert Quay on 11 July 1974.** Aubrey Dale

Lower right: **The approach to Albert Quay was through a cutting and a short tunnel. The rows of terraced houses on the opposite bank of the River Lee illustrate the hilly nature of Cork city.** Author

Lower left: **This was the view from the brake-van of a Cork City line train as it approached Albert Quay on 17 March 1961.** R. M. Casserley

Right: **The impressive stone buildings of Albert Quay station survive, and are seen here in December, 2001. The gates are those seen in the centre of the earlier view.** Author

Below: **This general view of Albert Quay shows the elevated signalbox behind which is the passenger station, out of sight, with the goods platforms to the right.** IRRS collection

Bottom: **At Albert Quay on 3 November 1960 are two AEC-engined Park Royal-bodied railcars, which took over virtually all the passenger workings in the last years of the West Cork lines.** John Langford

Above: **Three of the CB&SCR's most celebrated class of locomotives are seen grouped around the turntable at Albert Quay. The 4-6-0T was a most unusual wheel arrangement within the British Isles, but this railway had a fleet of them** built by Beyer Peacock. They were excellent machines and some migrated to suburban services south of Dublin. However, most remained on home territory, and here we see Nos 468, 463 and 470. A. F. Porter

Below: **GSR No 477, built by Dübs as a 2-4-0T in 1875 for the Cork & Bandon Railway, and converted to a 4-4-0T in 1908, is seen shunting alongside a tall-funnelled freighter on the dockside at Cork shortly before withdrawal in 1930.** Rex Murphy

Right: **No 12**, one of the line's Beyer Peacock 0-6-0STs, built in 1882, is at home at Rocksavage Depot, Cork, in CB&SCR days. The depot was situated in the open air, the only protection from the elements being the bridge behind the locomotive. The saddle tank was never re-numbered by the GSR, being broken up in 1925. Author's collection

Below: **No 5**, an almost identical 0-6-0ST of 1887, lasted rather longer. It is seen here, smoking and steaming nicely and flaunting its GSR number 475, around 1930. It was withdrawn in 1939. Author's collection

Right: **No 491 at Rocksavage on 10 June 1932.** This neat 2-4-2T was originally the Waterford, Limerick & Western Railway's No 13 *Derry Castle*, built by the Vulcan Foundry in 1891. On passing to the GS&WR it was renumbered 266, lost its name and was then sold to the Cork & Macroom Direct in 1914. Here it is numbered 6. Returning to the Inchicore fold in 1925, it survived as No 491 until 1934. H. C. Casserley

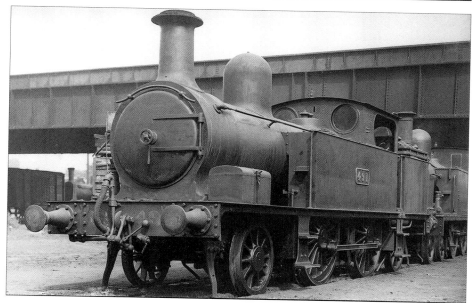

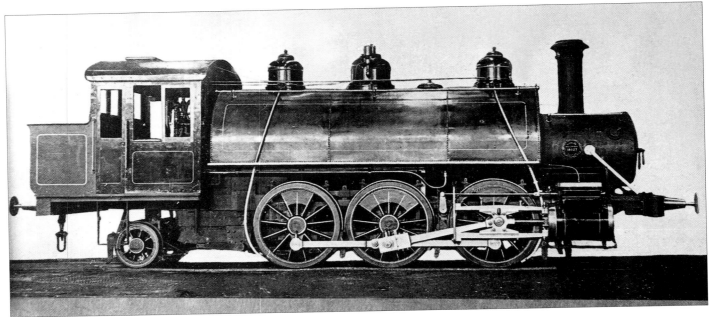

Above: **One of the oddest-looking locomotives ever to run in Ireland was this 0-6-2ST, one of two, Nos 19 and 20, built in 1900 by the Baldwin Locomotive Works in the USA, as British builders were too busy to accommodate the CB&SCR. Although of a standard design popular on the other side of the Atlantic, the orphans were scorned in Cork and both had gone by 1914. Until the advent of the CIE General Motors diesels in the 1950s, they were the only American locomotives to run in Ireland.** John Langford collection

Left: **It was not until Chetwynd Viaduct on the western outskirts of Cork city, seen here, and Gogginshill Tunnel were completed that the lines from West Cork were connected to Cork city in 1851. The train is a farewell special, organised by the IRRS and hauled by one of the CB&SCR 4-6-0Ts in March 1961.** Walter McGrath collection

Left: **A main-line train of bogie carriages, the 8.05am service from Bantry to Cork, hauled by 4-6-0T No 470, is seen on 21 September 1953 at Clonakilty Junction, where the Clonakilty and Courtmacsherry lines branched off from the Bantry line.** Neil Sprinks

Top: **No 201, an Ivatt 'J11' 0-6-0T of 1887, passes Clonakilty Junction with a down goods on 21 September 1953.** Neil Sprinks

Above: **A mixed train consisting of 2-4-2T No 35, another Ivatt locomotive of 1893, one six-wheel passenger Brake, one six-wheel Composite and a goods brake-van is seen at Clonakilty Junction on the same day.** Neil Sprinks

Right: **The 'C' class of Bo-Bo diesel-electrics took over working the West Cork branches in their final years. Here No C222 stands at Clonakilty Junction with the 11.00am mixed train for Clonakilty on 24 August 1957.** C. H. A. Townley

Top: **No C234 stands at Clonakilty Junction with a mixed train from Clonakilty on 14 September 1960.** R. N. Joanes

Above: **No 35 is seen again with its mixed train at the Clonakilty branch terminus on 21 September 1953.** Neil Sprinks

Left: **The Courtmacsherry branch left the Clonakilty line at Ballinascarthy, and a mixed train is seen here at a location known as Siberia. The locomotive is** *St Molaga*, **a diminutive 0-4-2T built by Hunslet in 1890 for the Timoleague & Courtmacsherry Extension Light Railway – a name almost as long as the line. The car is a brand-new Morris 8, which dates the picture to 1937/8.** W. A. Camwell

Above: **Another view of *St Molaga*, which never carried a number throughout its long career. Withdrawn in 1949, it is seen here at Cork in the 1930s.**
Kelland Collection

Right: ***Argadeen* was also built by Hunslet for the Timoleague & Courtmacsherry Extension Light Railway, in 1894, and was the only broad gauge 5ft 3in gauge 2-6-0T ever to operate in Ireland. It was fitted by the Great Southern with a boiler from a Dublin & South Eastern Railway railmotor – waste not, want not – and continued to serve the County Cork lines until 1957.**
Author's collection

Right: **At Courtmacsherry station on August Bank Holiday 1955 two small 0-6-0Ts, Nos 90 and 100, have manfully struggled in with their heavily laden train of elderly arc-roofed carriages conveying eager excursionists bound for the regatta. No 100 was built in 1891 and withdrawn in 1959, while No 90 was once the 'hot end' of an 0-6-4T railmotor. No 90 was preserved on withdrawal and spent many years on a plinth at Mallow Station.**
Cork Examiner

Above: **At Courtmacsherry on 25 August 1957, looking seawards, is another 0-6-0T, No 552, of Class J26, one of the very few classes of southern Irish tank engines to number more than half a dozen. There were 12 of them, designed by Atock for the Midland & Great Western Railway in 1891. The train is about to set off back to Cork city.** C. H. A. Townley

Left: **Further west was Drimoleague, the junction for Skibbereen, where 4-6-0T No 463 is seen shunting at the junction station on 21 September 1953.** Neil Sprinks

Below: **2-4-2T No 34, with an ex-GS&WR bogie coach and a six-wheeled passenger brake arrive at Drimoleague from Skibbereen on the same day.** Neil Sprinks

Above: **This is Skibbereen station in the late 1930s, with its substantial signalbox. A mixed train stands at the platform.** Author's collection

Right: **No 34 is resting over the ash pit in front of the engine shed at Skibbereen on 20 September 1953.** Neil Sprinks

Below: **Our final view of No 34 is at Skibbereen's station with a mixed train for Baltimore on 22 September 1953.** Neil Sprinks

Left: **The line from Skibbereen was extended to Baltimore in 1893. No 34 stands at the far end of the station, opposite the platform, on 21 September 1953.** Neil Sprinks

Centre left: **Broad gauge met narrow gauge at Skibbereen. This is the narrow gauge station on 1 July 1938; Schull & Skibbereen 4-4-0T No 4s is arriving with the 10.00am train from Schull prior to reversing into the platform.** H. C. Casserley

Below: **Later the same day No 4s took out the 12 noon train from Skibbereen. A trilby-hatted passenger looks out from carriage No 1s as the train pauses at Hollyhill.** H. C. Casserley

Above right: **A pony and trap is seen beside No 4s at Hollyhill on the same occasion.** H. C. Casserley

Below right: **No 4s takes on water in the remote setting of Crooked Bridge, approximately halfway between Skibbereen and Schull.** H. C. Casserley

Above: **No 4 stands alongside the platform at Ballydehob, two stations before the terminus at Schull. From this angle, with its cowcatcher and large headlamp, No 4 bears quite a transatlantic air, not inappropriate for a line that terminated close to the last landfall of New York-bound liners.** H. C. Casserley

Left: **By 1939 the railway was in dire straits from competition, with motor vehicles making use of the road that ran alongside the line for much of its length. The train is en route from Skibbereen.** W. A. Camwell

Below: **Although the Schull & Skibbereen Railway closed down completely in February 1947, Neil Sprinks found most of its rolling-stock still intact in September 1953. This is bogie carriage No 5s, standing amongst the grass at Skibbereen.** Neil Sprinks

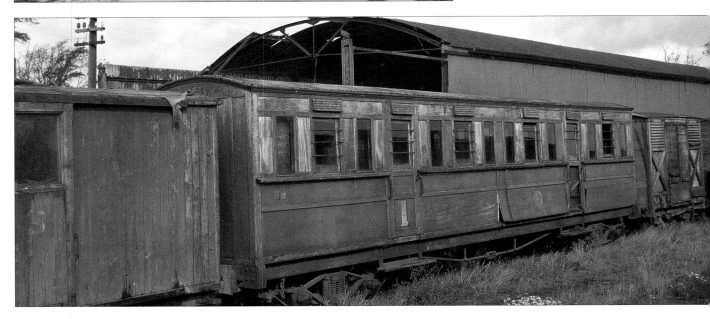

Top: **The CB&SCR 4-6-0Ts virtually monopolised traffic between Cork and Baltimore and Bantry until the end of steam; here one of them has charge of a Bantry-bound train in about 1925.** Author's collection

Above: **Deep in the West Cork countryside a westbound train composed of a mixture of bogie and six-wheel carriages and vans is in the charge of another 4-6-0T.** Author's collection

Right: **Looking down on Bantry station in CIE days, the inevitable 4-6-0T is standing ahead of the turntable, while a former GS&WR clerestory carriage stands at the platform. The railway swept around the town and made a 180-degree turn on its way westwards from Cork city.** Author's collection

Above: **Another view of Bantry station with the magnificent bay dominating the picture.** IRRS collection

Left: **Bantry at sunset on an August evening in 1996. The evening bus from Cork city has just arrived and stands beside the bay. Over to the right, out of sight, is where the station used to be. Bantry has changed little, visually, since the previous picture was taken.** Author

Below: **An 0-6-0ST and a 4-4-0T have charge of a train from Bantry as it arrives back at Albert Quay station in Cork in the late 1920s. The leading engine is a standard Beyer Peacock design of 1894 similar to a number bought by the London & South Western Railway.** Rex Murphy

CAPWELL TO MACROOM

Above: **Cork Capwell station was the city terminus of the Cork & Macroom Railway, and is seen here on 24 July 1914 with 2-4-0T No 4 departing for Macroom. Within a few short weeks this seemingly serene, everyday picture would belong to world gone for ever in Cork city and the country – the outbreak of World War 1, the events of 1916, much suffering in Cork city and the countryside, the death of the Lord Mayor, Terence MacSwiney, on hunger strike in Brixton prison, independence, the death of Michael Collins at Beal na mBlath west of Cork city, and, in 1935, the end of passenger traffic on the Cork & Macroom. No 4 was a Dübs engine dating from 1881, and lasted but three years with the Great Southern, being withdrawn as No 489 in 1928.** Ken Nunn Collection

Centre right: **Macroom station in the 1930s, with a very natty gent in the foreground and a porter with a broom in the background.** Stations UK

Right: **Southern Motorways began to operate buses over the 24 miles between Cork and Macroom in 1927. Its daily weekday service of nine journeys in each direction was in competition with the rail-sponsored Irish Omnibus Company, so it is not surprising that passenger services on the line were withdrawn in 1935. Goods service survived until 1953, and one of the last cattle specials is seen here, on 10 November 1953, being shunted on the overgrown tracks at Macroom by GS&WR 2-4-2T No 36 just before the end.** Walter McGrath

Above: **2-4-2T No 33 is being prepared for the very last train on the Macroom line on 10 November 1953.** Author's collection

Below: **The railway is still remembered in Macroom today, and some of the railway buildings still exist, being used by Bus Eireann.** Author

Below: **Buses now have a monopoly of public transport to the west and north of Cork city. A Bus Eireann coach heads along the quays in Cork in December 2001.** Author

WESTERN ROAD

Right: **Not many Irish railways had a city station built on an island, but that's where Western Road, the terminus of the Cork & Muskerry Light Railway, was situated, in the South Channel of the River Lee. One of its dinky little 0-4-4Ts, No 5K, built by Greens of Leeds – not a particularly well-known firm – is setting off for Coachford on 15 September 1929.** H. C. Casserley

Right: **No 6K, the other Green 0-4-4T, stands on the turntable at Western Road. One wonders how much the light above the engineman — who is not quite sure whether he is supposed to be in the picture or not — would have cast on the proceedings once night fell. No 6K survived the closure of its native line in 1934, being sent westwards to the Schull & Skibbereen, where it became 6S and survived until 1954.** Author's collection

Below left: **A train headed by a 4-4-0T, rebuilt from a 2-4-0T, approaches Western Road, passing a gentleman on a bicycle and what looks very like a Corporation Shelvoke & Drewry dust cart on 10 June 1932.** H. C. Casserley

Below right: **One of the railway's branch lines served Blarney and its famous castle, in competition with the Great Southern & Western. Thus it was not surprising that one of its original Kitson-built 0-4-2Ts was so named. Unfortunately it was a lot less long-lived than its predecessor, being underpowered, and was sold in 1910.** IAL

GLANMIRE ROAD

Left: **I first visited Cork in 1959, 6 September to be precise, arriving in a cattle lorry, having hitch-hiked from Waterford by way of all sorts of interesting diversions deep into the Cork countryside. I was immediately smitten by the Republic's second city, splendidly situated in the bright, late summer afternoon sunshine along the banks of the River Lee and set amongst hills with church spires dominating the skyline, as can be seen in this view taken in the late 1950s looking down the astonishingly steep St Patrick's Hill to the city centre. Amongst the traffic are CIE Tiger and Titan buses.** Deegan-Photo

Centre left: **Some 50 years earlier this is the view from St Patrick's Bridge looking back up the hill away from the city centre. A couple of trams, which ran from 1898 to 1931, are crossing the bridge.** Commercial postcard

Below: **When I first visited Cork there was still plenty of steam locomotives to be seen. Cork had a busy shed full of locomotives. From left to right they are 'J15' 0-6-0 No 108, ahead of a 'J26' 0-6-0T, a Woolwich 2-6-0, 'J26' No 552, 'B4' Bandon tank 4-6-0T No 470 and, lurking behind the telegraph pole, 0-6-0T No 100.** Author

Above right: **A far less well-known class of 4-6-0 was Coey's GS&WR inside-cylinder goods engines of 1905. No 364 is seen here at Cork when fairly new. The six members of the class were not very successful, being no great improvement on the 2-6-0s and the bigger 0-6-0s. They were withdrawn in 1928-31.** IAL

Right: **No 38 stands at the southern end of Glanmire Road station in the 1930s. This Ivatt-designed 'C7' class 4-4-2T was one of a pair of suburban tank engines dating from 1894. It was withdrawn in 1950.** Author's collection

Below: **Taken at the same location but on a track nearer the camera, a Tralee to Cobh excursion heads through Glanmire Road on 8 July 1934 in the charge of No 336, a Coey 'D4' of 1907, and 'J15' No 129 of 1889. The stock is a mixture of six-wheeled and bogie carriages, mostly in the GSR chocolate-and-cream livery introduced in the late 1920s, although the leading six-wheeler is still in the former claret.** H. C. Casserley

Above: 4-6-0 No 406 has just arrived at Cork with an express from Dublin in about 1950. On conversion from four to two cylinders in May 1930, she was fitted with Caprotti valve gear, as can be clearly seen in this picture. That authority on Irish steam locomotives, Bob Clements said she was now 'very satisfactory' although 'compared to the very reliable 402 (which also had Caprotti gear), 406 always seemed a bit temperamental.' No 406 was withdrawn in March 1957. Author's collection

Below: Glanmire Road station, which in common with other main stations in the Irish Republic, were renamed after leaders of the 1916 Rebellion, is called Kent station. Re-engined Metro-Vickers 'A' class Co-Co No A29R stands in front of the carriage sheds at the south end of the station in August 1974. Author

Above: **Metro-Vickers Co-Co No A7 shunts empty stock at the south end of Kent Station on Saturday 26 April 1969. In the engine shed yard is preserved former NCC 2-6-4T No 4, which had brought in the 'Brian Boru' Railway Preservation Society of Ireland rail tour.** A. W. Nokes

Right: **No 203, a General Motors 2,300hp Co-Co, stands at Cork Kent station, with the docks in the background, having arrived with the 07.30 service from Dublin in December 2001.** Author

Left: '201' class locomotive, No 228, passes the signalbox at the south end of Kent station. Author

Below: The impressive stone goods shed situated between Kent passenger station and the docks, Cork, in 1969. To the right is No B102, one of the Birmingham/Sulzer A1A-A1A locomotives, standing on the track which carried freight trains across the city to Albert Quay Author

Left: *Pat* was one of the sights of Cork. This curiosity was a vertical-boilered 0-4-0T built at Inchicore in 1884, probably using an ancient outside-frame tender as chassis, and spent its long career (it was scrapped as late as 1963) shunting coal from ships on Penrose Quay along its own 380yd-long line to the coal bunkers at Cork shed. It did not normally carry its name so prominently, but was being visited, shortly before withdrawal, by members of the IRRS. Walter McGrath

CORK TO MALLOW

Right: **Most trains tackling the fearsome 1 in 78/64 northwards through the damp tunnel out of Glanmire Road station needed to be double-headed. Here the 'Rosslare Express' is about to depart in about 1907 behind a 'J15' 0-6-0 No 188 of 1882 and No 312, a Coey 'D10' class 4-4-0 of 1903.** IAL

Right: **By 1959 most of the Great Southern 4-6-0s, Ireland's one group of really big engines, had gone for scrap, so I was most delighted to find that one of the three still surviving, No 402, was rostered for the overnight Dublin goods. I took up position beside Glanmire Road station, with a view of the curving double track that ran round the back of the station. My patience was eventually rewarded as a shrill whistle sounded above the noise of the road traffic and the 'J15' shunting cattle trucks along the dockside, and the beat of a big two-cylinder engines heralded No 402 getting a grip of her long train of unbraked wagons. She thundered past me and into the tunnel and away towards Mallow. She and her surviving sister, No 401, were withdrawn in March 1961.** Author

Right: **Two years later much to my astonishment I came across No 801 *Macha*, one of the two survivors of the 'Queen' class 4-6-0s, built in the late 1930s and early 1940s to haul the Dublin to Cork mail trains. Despite long replaced from top link activities by diesels and to all intents and purposes being redundant she was still in immaculate condition. No 801 is seen here climbing effortlessly up the 1 in 63 out of Glanmire Road tunnel with a lightweight goods train for Thurles. A few month later, in 1962, she was withdrawn whilst her surviving sister, No 800 *Maeve*, was towed across the border to preservation and display at Cultra.** Author

Above: **By the early 1960s diesels had made great inroads into steam, surprisingly, one 4-6-0 still remained – No 801 *Macha*. CIE really had no need of her, and, based at Thurles, she pottered around on light goods duties way beneath the dignity of what had once been Ireland's finest. The 'B1a' class had very little opportunity to show their paces as Ireland's premier express passenger locomotives; the 'A' class diesels took over the Dublin-Cork passenger trains in 1955, railcars having appeared on the route several years earlier, and No 802 ceased work in January 1956, being** broken up a year or so later. No 800 was taken out of service at the end of 1958 and might well have suffered the same fate as No 802, but the Irish Railway Record Society persuaded Dr C S Andrews, the Chairman of CIE, that this most famous of locomotives deserved a better fate. Transport preservation was a low priority with CIE in those days, but *Maedhbh* did survive. In 1964 she was towed north, where the authorities were rather more sympathetic, and today can be seen, a splendid sight, in the magnificent Transport Museum at Cultra, outside Belfast. No 801 was withdrawn a few months later and was broken up at Inchicore. In happier days one of the 'B1' class 4-6-0s passes the sidings at Rathpeacon with an up express, seen from the cab of a Cork-bound train, in about 1950. There were extensive sidings here, as can be seen, where wagons were stored and remarshalled.**
Author's collection

Below: **'J15' 0-6-0 No 193 arrives at Blarney with a down stopping train on 9 July 1934. Long closed, Blarney station is due to re-open in the near future.**
H. C. Casserley

Above: **Mallow has a key role in our story for it is here that the line to Killarney and Tralee, Kerry's last surviving rail link diverges from the Dublin to Cork main line. It was also the junction for the line from Rosslare and Waterford. This is the view looking northwards on 10 June 1958 with the Waterford line swinging to the right beyond the signalbox.** A. E. Bennett

ight: **A Great Southern Railway guard at Mallow in 1933.** Father Francis Browne

Above: **One of the pioneer CIE 915hp Bo-Bo diesel locomotives, No 1101 of 1951, stands at Mallow with the 12.30pm Dublin Kingsbridge to Cork train on 26 September 1953. The notion of a horsebox and such a lightweight train on** the Dublin to Cork main line would seem inconceivable in 2005. Neil Sprinks

Below: **On the same day the 5.40pm Cork to Rosslare Harbour train rolls into Mallow behind Woolwich Mogul No 394.** It is heading a boat train that will connect with an overnight sailing to Fishguard, from whence a British Railways Western Region express will deposit the weary traveller at Paddington in the early hours of the morning. Neil Sprinks

Above: **The distinctive awning of Mallow station, dating from Victorian times, is seen here in 1996. My wife's grandmother told me that her grandmother, who lived at Mallow, was taken as a child to see Queen Victoria when she came to Ireland in 1859. The train stopped overnight in the station and she saw Prince Albert pull back** the curtains of the carriage window so that the Queen could look out at the assembled crowds and wave at them. Author

Below: **4-6-0 No 500 pulls out of Mallow with the Cork-bound Day Mail, with two vans – one bogie, one six-wheeled – leading. No 500, built in 1924, was the** first of three 4-6-0s, designed as mixed-traffic engines. However, they proved perfectly capable of working main line passenger trains and, with the disappointing performance of the 'B2' class, the 'B1s' spent more than 30 years hauling expresses between Dublin and Cork. P. Ward

Above: **The Killarney-bound 'Radio Train', hauled by rebuilt GS&WR 4-6-0 No 402 of 1921, approaches Mallow on 15 June 1954. The 'Radio Train' was a popular tourist attraction, an excursion from Dublin with music, commentary and refreshments provided in both directions and a trip by jaunting car around the lakes on arrival at Killarney. In Edwardian times the Great Western** Railway advertised a similar day excursion – although in reality it took nearer two – all the way from Paddington, crossing from Fishguard to Rosslare overnight, train to Killarney, then back overnight, arriving in London in time for breakfast. P. Ward

Below: **Another 'Radio Train', with its distinctive headboard, swings across to the up line beyond Mallow station, ready to take the Kerry turnout and head towards Killarney. The immaculate green-painted locomotive, No 405, was built in 1923 and withdrawn in 1955. Most of the carriages are wooden-bodied vehicles dating back to the 1920s and beyond.** B. Williams

LINES AROUND MALLOW

Right: **The most serious accident to befall the railways of Ireland in the last decades of the 20th century occurred at Buttevant, between Mallow and Charleville, on 1 August 1980. The heavily loaded 12-coach 12.40 Dublin to Cork express, hauled by General Motors Co-Co locomotive No 075, was passing at speed through the station when the driver found that the points were set for the goods yard. He could do nothing to reduce his speed, and the heavy locomotive continued on in a more or less straight line and eventually came to a halt, upright, relatively undamaged. The vehicle immediately behind the locomotive, all-steel modified BR Mk 1 SV heating guards van No 3191, lost its bogies but the body remained largely intact. However, the following three carriages, two dining-cars and a 1st, of wooden-framed steel-sided construction, were demolished, and in them 18 people died. The Cravens carriages in the train sustained relatively little damage. As the Journal of the Irish Railway Record Society commented, 'There can be little doubt that if sufficient up-to-date rolling-stock of integral body construction, equipped with the buck-eye type of couplings, and with anti-collision gangways, had been included in the assembly of the train the consequences would have been much less severe.' This aerial view graphically conveys the awful scene.** Irish Press

Centre right: **Three weeks later work is still going on putting the track to rights. The generator van No 3191 has been re-bogied and stands in the siding, and immediately ahead of it are the points that caused the derailment, while behind the motor van in the yard is the piled up wreckage of the carriages.** Author

Lower right: **Fermoy, east of Mallow and the junction for the Mitchelstown branch, is seen here on 15 June 1954. No 334, a Coey 'D4' 4-4-0 of 1907, stands outside the impressive overall roof with a train from Mallow.** C. H. A. Townley

Above: **On 28 March 1963 Fermoy is host to a fascinating mix of motive power. On the left is Metro-Vickers 'A' class No A11 in original green livery with a goods train, beside it stands General Motors No B141, while in the bay platform is now preserved 0-6-0T No 90.** R. N. Joanes

Left: **From Fermoy, a branch headed north to Mitchelstown. At the branch terminus on 22 June 1939, No 15, a McDonnell 4-4-0 of 1880, rebuilt with a Belpaire boiler, is ready to depart with the 4.15pm train for Fermoy.** W. A. Camwell

Left: **On the line west from Mallow into Kerry, at Banteer seen here on 10 June 1958, a branch struck off to Newmarket.** A E Bennett

Above right: **The very elderly No 7, a McDonnell 4-4-0 of 1877, is in charge of the two six-wheelers that make up the branch train at Newmarket station in 1939. No 7 was not withdrawn until 1953.** W. A. Camwell

Right: **'D19' No 7 is seen outside Newmarket's single road engine shed on the same date.** W. A. Camwell

KERRY

Across the border in County Kerry the extension from Killarney to Tralee was opened on Sunday 16 July 1859. Owned by a separate company, it was taken over by the Great Southern & Western the following year. The junction at Killarney was, and is, far from convenient, trains from the Mallow direction having to run into the station, then reverse out to resume their progress westwards, curving sharply away to run past the back of the town. The great Irish civil engineer, William Dargan, built both the Mallow to Killarney line and the extension on to Tralee. The opening of the Mallow to Killarney line took place in the immediate aftermath of the Famine. Commemorating the centenary of the opening of the line to Killarney in June 1953, the *Kerryman* noted that 'Kerry was a county of starvation. Gaunt men, emaciated from hunger, tried to work for a few pence a day, not to bring the railway to Killarney, but to keep their homes together'. One hundred years earlier the *Kerry Evening Post* recorded that 'the working people of Millstreet and Killarney are now well fed and clothed where before they went hungry and naked'.

At the opposite extreme of the social scale, and what must have seemed to some in conditions of almost obscene contrast, Queen Victoria and Prince Albert visited Killarney travelling in a magnificently appointed conveyance in August 1849. Not surprisingly, whatever their political views, the visit was long remembered by the local population.

Initially the journey between Killarney and Dublin took more than eight hours, which nevertheless did much to combat the sense of isolation that until then prevailed in the west, while by the end of the century this time had been halved. Today the 08.30 train from Dublin reaches Killarney in 3½ hours. Beyond Mallow the line is, and always has been, single track.

The railway proved a huge boon to the tourist industry. Thomas Cook first included Killarney in its programme in 1895, a group from the USA stayed at the Great Southern hotel in 1896, and in 1906 the opening of the Fishguard to Rosslare shipping service encouraged the Great Western Railway, part owners of the Rosslare to Mallow route, to run excursions from Paddington. The excursionists arrived at Fishguard from Paddington at 2.30 on the Saturday morning and crossed to Rosslare. A special train then took them direct to Killarney, whence they were taking by jaunting car to view the lakes and mountains, and they arrived back, hopefully fulfilled if exhausted, in London early on Sunday morning. The construction of the railway may have provided much-needed labouring work, but 3rd Class passengers were not encouraged and their only train of the day at the opening of the railway took 12 hours to reach Killarney from Dublin. However, they were not discouraged, the directors came to their senses, and by 1913 no less than 93% of all tickets sold were for 3rd Class.

Various branches followed the opening of the line to Killarney and Tralee. The first train ran from Headford Junction to Kenmare on 4 September 1893, that from Farranfore to Valencia, the most westerly point of the European railway network, on 12 August 1893, Gortatlea to Castleisland on 30 August 1875, from Tralee to Fenit on 5 July 1887, from

Below left: **There are many hand-operated level-crossing gates on the Mallow to Tralee line, and here is an Iarnrod Eireann sign at one of them in August 2004. The chances of collision with a steam engine were fairly remote by this date.** Author

Below: **Semaphore signals still predominated in 2004, and this one was photographed just down the line from the previous picture.** Author

Tralee to Newcastle (the North Kerry line) on 20 December 1880, thus completing the through route from Tralee to Limerick, while the narrow-gauge line from Tralee to Dingle, with a branch to Castlegregory, started operation on 1 April 1891. Finally, the extraordinary Lartigue monorail between Listowel and Ballybunion was inaugurated on 5 March 1888.

All of these were to close, elderly residents often commenting as the last train left their local station that they could remember the first. The Kenmare branch ceased on 1 January 1960, and the Valencia branch closed one month later, except for a cattle specials, which ran until that summer. The Castleisland branch closed on 10 January 1977. The Fenit line closed officially on 2 June 1978, although it was partly refurbished by the now defunct GSR Preservation Society in the mid-1980s. The North Kerry line shut down section by section, goods traffic on the final remaining section, between Abbeydorney and Tralee, ceasing on 2 June 1978. On the narrow gauge, the Castlegregory branch shut down on 17 April 1939, as did the passenger service between Tralee and Dingle. Goods services survived until 10 March 1947, while monthly cattle trains ran until 1 July 1953. However, the Tralee & Dingle refused to die, and on 10 July 1993 1¼ miles came back to life when the section from Tralee Ballyard to Blennerville re-opened. The Listowel to Ballybunion monorail was, perhaps inevitably, the first section of railway in County Kerry to close, on 14 October 1924. But even more remarkable than the revival of the Tralee & Dingle has been that of the Lartigue, and the 21st century – 2003 to be precise – saw a section once more in operation at Listowel.

The network of routes in County Kerry gave employment right until the end of steam to elderly 4-4-0s and the ever faithful maids of all work, the 'J15' ('101') class 0-6-0s most suitable for these lightly laid lines. Large locomotives, the Woolwich 2-6-0s and the '400' and '500' series 4-6-0s, were seen as far west as Killarney. This tourist honeypot has always provided the railways with good business, although the traffic has never been as great as that on the Cork line. Once beyond Mallow, single track has always been the order of the day throughout Kerry, a good indication of the relative sparseness of services.

The 2005 timetable shows through trains, Monday to Saturday, from Dublin Heuston to Tralee at 8.30 and 18.30. Trains in the other direction leave Tralee at 07.00 and 14.00. They take between four and four and three quarter hours. In the down direction there are connections at Mallow to Tralee out of the 07.10, 10.55, 13.00, 15.20, and 17.00 Dublin to Cork services. In the up direction there are connections at Mallow with Dublin trains off the 09.15, 16.00 and 18.00 Tralee to Cork services. Two through trains run between Tralee and Cork, at 16.00 and 18.00, this journey taking around two and a half hours. Trains leave Cork for Tralee at 13.00, 15.05 and 17.10. There are also connections at Mallow for the Cork line. A recent innovation has been two railcar-operated trains from Killarney to Cork at 06.30 and 11.15, Monday to Saturday, returning from Cork 09.10 and 18.45.

'201' class locomotives haul the through Dublin-Cork trains, whilst the now elderly and disappearing smaller Bo-Bo GMs have charge of Craven carriages, for the moment although not for much longer, on the Tralee, Killarney to Cork services.

Until the beginning of 2005 Killarney possessed a magnificent array of semaphore signals — Oliver Doyle in his article in the June 2005 edition of *Irish Railway News* describes it as 'the finest in Ireland' — but Central Train Control (CTC) was inaugurated between Banteer and Tralee on 25 February and there are now no semaphore signals between Tralee and Mallow, although some signalboxes remain, temporarily, to control some of the many level crossings between Banteer and Tralee. This means that there is CTC all the way from Dublin to Tralee and Dublin to Cork. Traditional methods with a good few semaphores interspersed with colour lights still pertain between Cork and Cobh. In connection with changes to the signalling, the opportunity was also taken to carry out various improvements, especially at Killarney where the bay and mainline platforms were extended, the junction known as the Check Road on account of tickets being checked at a platform here in the days of non-corridor stock was moved back and two crossovers lengthened to speed up the progress of trains negotiating them. Killarney, much the busiest station between Mallow and Tralee, is a terminus and all trains from Tralee have to back in, whilst those from Mallow have to reverse out before continuing westwards. At various places between Mallow and Tralee the tracks have been realigned and any remaining sidings removed, freight trains, sadly, being a thing of the past. Punctuality on the Dublin to Tralee route, not always very good, has of late improved and reached 90% in January 2005. That for the Dublin to Cork line was 91.4%.

Finally, let us salute Killarney station's award of Best Floral Display on the Irish Rail network in 2004, and Mallow, my wife's ancestral home, coming top of the entire class with 'Best Overall Station' and being presented with the Waterford Wedgewood trophy.

HEADFORD AND THE KENMARE BRANCH

Right: **The caption for this official picture is 'Modern CIE train at Headford, Co Kerry'. The date stamp says 1969, but that can't be correct for it also says 'CIE Kingsbridge', and the HQ had become Heuston in 1966. Re-engining of the 'A' class had begun in 1968 so it seems unlikely that one of the unrebuilt examples, No A6, would have been chosen. The four-wheel heating and guard's vans were something of an anachronism, although they remained in use well into the 1970s. The fourth vehicle is the State Saloon, No 351, now superbly restored and repainted in GS&WR livery.** CIE

Top: 'D11' class No 301 has charge of a Tralee to Dublin train at Headford Junction on 12 July 1934. The Kenmare branch train is on the left in the branch platform. H. C. Casserley

Above: On 11 June 1958 No C210 enters the station with a train off the Kenmare branch. A. E. Bennett

Left: No 714, one of the 'J15B' 0-6-0s of 1934 that were intended to be an improved version of the 'J15s' but proved to be a good deal more feeble, rolls into Headford Junction with an up freight on 22 September 1953. Note the locomotive's ancient outside-frame tender. No 714 lasted a mere 25 years, hardly a sound investment compared to one of its GS&WR predecessors.
Neil Sprinks

Top: **Not a view available to your average passenger, this photograph was taken from an open wagon in a mixed train pausing at Morley's Bridge on its way to Kenmare on 11 June 1958. A bogie carriage has been provided at the front of the train for the not excessive number of passengers.** A. E. Bennett

Above: **'J15' No 127 stands in Kenmare station with the 9.30am train to Headford Junction consisting of one bogie and two six-wheeled carriages, on 23 September 1953.** Neil Sprinks

Lower right: **The corrugated-iron station building at Kenmare, photographed on 11 June 1958. It may not figure particularly high in the ranks of railway architectural gems, but its immaculate condition is a credit to the staff. The spire of the parish church can be seen above the trees in the distance. The branch closed to all traffic on 1 January 1960.** A. E. Bennett

KILLARNEY

Left: **The 09.15 Tralee to Dublin express, headed by a GM '201' class Co-Co and composed of BR-built air-conditioned stock, accelerates away from Killarney in August 2004.** Author

Below: **The 'Radio Train' approaches Killarney headed by one of the original General Motors single-cab '121' class Bo-Bos in August 1975.** Author's collection

Bottom: **In this view from the main platform of Killarney station on 3 June 1958, looking towards Mallow, Metro-Vickers 'A' class Co-Co No A36 stands at the head of the 'Radio Train', attached to a 'tin van' the colloquial term applied to these four-wheeled heating vans, designed by Oliver Bulleid during his time as CME at CIE in the 1950s.** John Langford

Above: **General Motors Bo-Bo No B153 is about to depart from Killarney with the 10.05 Tralee to Dublin train on 25 June 1970.** H. W. Cater

Centre left: **The foyer of the very grand Great Southern Hotel in August 2004, built by the Great Southern & Western Railway. An advertisement at the turn of the 20th century for the hotel informed passengers that it was 'connected with the Railway Station by a private covered way. The most commodious and best appointed Hotel in the Lake District . . . Conveyances leave the Hotel at about 9.30am daily during the season for the Grand Tour of the Gap of Dunloe and the three Lakes, Muckross Abbey, Derrycunihy Falls, and other principal routes. The Hotel Porters, in uniform, meet all Trains for the conveyance of Luggage between the Hotel and the Railway Station, free of charge.' There was obviously no shortage of capital letters in Killarney in Edwardian times.** Author

Centre right: **A GWR poster advertising travel to Southern Ireland.** Author

Lower right: **Passengers from the 'Radio Train' climb aboard jaunting cars for a tour of the Lakes of Killarney in the early 1970s. So popular was, and is, Killarney that the Great Western Railway organised what it called a day excursion from Paddington by way of Fishguard and Rosslare, although it actually stretched over three days.** Author

Left: **A rake of elderly condemned CIE carriages, mostly six-wheelers of GS&WR and MGWR origin, await breaking up on the outskirts of Killarney on 10 June 1958.** A. E. Bennett

Above: **One of the Woolwich 2-6-0s approaches Killarney in about 1950 with a Tralee to Dublin train. These were by some distance the largest steam locomotives to work the line. Designed by R. E. L. Maunsell, once of the GS&WR, for the South Eastern & Chatham Railway, but built by the British Government at Woolwich for service after the 1914-18 war and subsequently bought as a kit of parts by the Midland Great Western Railway, these sturdy Moguls were erected in Dublin and were much valued by the GSR and CIE.** Author's collection

Left: **General Motors Bo-Bo No B156 approaches Killarney with a Tralee to Cork train in August 1969.** Author's collection

Right: **A Tralee to Dublin express approaching Killarney in August 1969 hauled by a General Motors Bo-Bo. The first and third carriages date from the 1950s, the second is a Great Southern Railway dining car built in the 1930s and fitted with CIE in the 1950s with B4 bogies. The following picture, dating from 2004, was taken from the bridge beneath which the train is passing.** Author

Below: **Killarney in August 2004, beyond the bridge. The 13.50 (Sundays only) Tralee to Dublin train is approaching Killarney. The town lies behind the trees, and beyond are the towering hills marking the beginning of the Ring of Kerry. The signal is in the same position as in the photograph of the Woolwich Mogul, although no longer with a lattice post.** Author

FARRANFORE AND THE VALENCIA BRANCH

Left: **Farranfore station in August 2004 looking towards Tralee. This was at one time the junction for the Valencia branch, the most westerly line in Europe. All the semaphore signals between Mallow and Tralee disappeared early in 2005 when CTC was introduced.** Author

Below: **The view from the GS&WR footbridge at Farranfore in August 2004, looking towards Tralee. The main Killarney to Tralee road crosses the railway here.** Author

Left: **On 24 September 1953 the 3.50pm Tralee to Valencia Harbour train arrives at Killorglin on the Valencia branch behind 'J15' No 126. It consists of two six-wheeled and two bogie carriages.** Neil Sprinks

Right: **Metro-Vickers Bo-Bo No C218 (left) has charge of the 3.35pm Tralee to Valencia Harbour train at Killorglin on 3 June 1958, while No C223 approaches with the 2.30pm service from Valencia Harbour to Tralee. These underpowered, unreliable 550hp locomotives were bought with such branch-line duties in mind, but branch lines were rapidly disappearing and the 'C' class would need re-engining by General Motors to turn them into useful machines. No C202, which worked the last service trains on the branch in January 1960, has been restored to its original silver livery and number, and can be seen on display at the Cahirciveen Heritage Centre.** John Langford

Above: **The bowstring girder viaduct over the River Laune at Killorglin, with its three 105ft spans, still survives in 2005, 45 years after the last train, a cattle special, passed over it.** Author

Above right: **The substantial stone-built Killorglin station, dating from 1885, has been converted to business premises.** Author

Right: **The trackbed of the Valencia Harbour branch near Dooks in August 2004.** Author

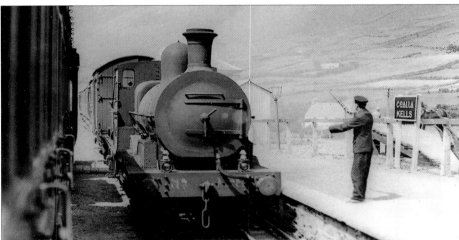

Above: **'J15' No 126 has charge of the 3.50pm Tralee to Valencia Harbour train at Glenbeigh station on 23 September 1953.** Neil Sprinks

Left: **The signalman at Kells station prepares to hand the single-line staff to the driver of the 'J15' No 128 as the train pulls in on 11 July 1934.** H. C. Casserley

Below: **A view of Kells station, looking back towards Farranfore, seen from a modern steel-sided CIE-built carriage on 10 June 1958.** A. E. Bennett

Right: **The 09.07am train from Killorglin to Valencia Harbour rolls across the impressive viaduct at Cahirciveen in the charge of 'J15' No 156 on 24 September 1953.** Neil Sprinks

Below: **Valencia Harbour, the most westerly station in Europe, photographed in July 1934.** H. C. Casserley

Bottom: **No 156, a 'J15' class 0-6-0, stands at Valencia Harbour station with the 2.10pm to Tralee on 24 September 1953.** Neil Sprinks

GORTATLEA AND THE CASTLEISLAND BRANCH

Left: **A view of Gortatlea seen from a train arriving from Killarney on 11 June 1958. The Castleisland branch trails in from the right, and a rake of withdrawn six-wheelers is sitting in the sidings.** A. E. Bennett

Left: **A goods train arriving at Gortatlea from Tralee hauled by 'J15' class 0-6-0 No 182 on 13 July 1934.** H. C. Casserley

Below: **General Motors No B144 shunts the Castleisland branch goods at Gortatlea in August 1974. Although both passenger and goods traffic ended in 1947, regular freight traffic was re-instated in January 1957 and did not finally cease until January 1977.** Author

Opposite, top right: **With No B144 having moved further back, we can now see the derelict, overgrown island platform with the disused main-line station buildings at Gortatlea beyond, having closed in 1963.** Author

Below: **No B144 is seen again at the other end of the 4¼-mile branch, shunting vans at Castleisland in August 1974. I travelled out in the cab of the locomotive and went back in the guard's van. The local travel agent still had a faded poster advertising regular sailings from Cobh to New York by United States Lines.** Author

Bottom: **Seven months later re-engined 'A' class No 053 finds itself with plenty of business at Castleisland, making up the 12.30 departure to Tralee on 20 March 1975.** Aubrey Dale

Left: **Many years earlier, Castleisland station is seen during the 1930s with an 0-6-0T in charge of the two six wheelers, which look as if they are of MGWR origin, forming the branch train.** IAL

Below: **This time a former GS&WR 0-4-4WT, No 47, has charge of the branch train. The first carriage is a former GS&WR four-compartment Composite built in the 1880s with a lavatory for the lucky 1st Class passengers in the centre, the second a Brake 3rd of similar vintage with, to use a Desmond Coakham phrase, belt-and-braces provision of both side and roof lookouts.** Author's collection

Bottom: **Back on the main line, the 2.20pm Mallow to Tralee train is composed of a mixed variety of bogie carriages in the charge of 'D4' 4-4-0 No 336 of 1907, is seen west of Gortatlea on 25 September 1953.** Neil Sprinks

Right: **On the same day 'J15' No 126 is seen near Gortatlea with the 3.50pm Tralee to Valencia Harbour train, composed of rather more antiquated stock.** Neil Sprinks

Right: **General Motors Bo-Bo No 157 is close to the location of the previous picture with the 16.00 Mallow to Tralee train on 17 August 1977. The leading vehicle is one of the 'Dutch' heating vans built at Dundalk in 1961.** Author

Below: **Co-Co No 047 heads towards Gortatlea on the same day with the 17.10 Tralee to Dublin service, passing a fine display of telegraph poles.** Author

TRALEE

Left: **On 31 January 1953 the 3.45pm train to Valencia Harbour, composed of 'J15' No 187 with an outside-frame tender and a rake of elderly six-wheeled carriages, leaves Tralee past an impressive former GS&WR clerestory corridor composite dating from the first decade of the 20th century.** Neil Sprinks

Left: **'D2' 4-4-0 No 333 of 1907 has charge of the 1.20pm Mallow train at Tralee on 23 September 1953. No 333 was withdrawn in 1955.** Neil Sprinks

Below: **Tralee motive power depot is seen on 3 November 1960, well into the diesel era but still home to 'J26' 0-6-0T No 560 and a somewhat delicate-looking steam crane.** John Phillips

Left: **In Tralee yard on a Sunday morning in August 1974 are two very contrasting rakes of vehicles. On the left is the set of almost new BR-built Mk 2 air-conditioned carriages ('Super Trains' as the publicity department gushingly described them) that will form the afternoon departure to Dublin, while on the right is a line of cattle trucks, once a very common sight on Irish railways but soon to disappear.** Author

Top left: **Two small boys watch a re-engined Metro-Vickers Co-Co shunting Tralee's Rock Street yard, west of the passenger station, in August 1978.** Author's collection

Top right: **The west yard at Tralee, between Edward Street and Rock Street crossings, in August 1974.** Author

Centre right: **The end of the line: the buffer stops at Tralee in August, 2004. The right-hand rust-encrusted track continues over the level crossing and once took trains past an extensive goods yard and on to the North Kerry line and the Fenit branch.** Author

Right: **In the station forecourt at Tralee in August 1974 are two CIE 'E' class Leopard buses bound for Listowel and Dingle, destinations once served by the railway.** Author

TRALEE & DINGLE RAILWAY

Right: **On the 3ft-gauge Tralee & Dingle Railway, Hunslet 2-6-0T No 8T heads out of the Tralee & Dingle station towards the main line to take on coal on 30 January 1953.** Neil Sprinks

Below: **These handsome stone buildings, photographed in the 1970s, were once the narrow-gauge railway's Tralee terminus.** Author

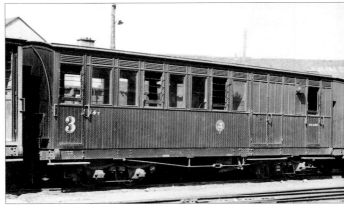

Above right: **Passenger traffic on the line ended in 1939. The carriages, all bogie vehicles, were divided internally into two sections, with seats along the sides in the longer section, and transverse seats in the** shorter. **The 3rd Class seats were wooden, the 1st Class ones upholstered. This is Brake 3rd No 14T at Tralee on 14 July 1934.** H. C. Casserley

Below: **Nos 8T and 1T take their cattle empties through Annascaul 30 January 1953.** Neil Sprinks

Above left: **Because of weight restrictions over Lispole Viaduct double-headed trains were not allowed, so No 1T works the cattle train alone, No 8T having already crossed to wait behind the camera where it will resume its duties.** Neil Sprinks

Above right: **On 28 July 1951, 2-6-0Ts Nos 1T and 2T struggle up the 1 in 29 gradient out of Lispole.** W. A. Aspell

Left: **Plenty of smoke and steam wreathes the shed to let the citizens of Dingle, down the hill, know that the railway is still in business. Nos 1T and 8T are being prepared to take an up cattle special on 31 January 1953.** Neil Sprinks

Below: **The same pair of locomotives shunt at Dingle prior to departing with the cattle special for Tralee on the same day.** Neil Sprinks

Above: **The cattle special has reached Castlegregory Junction on 31 January 1953, in a scene that perfectly portrays the glorious, sparsely populated landscape through which the Tralee & Dingle worked, and which hastened its demise.** Neil Sprinks

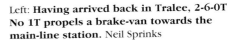

Left: **Having arrived back in Tralee, 2-6-0T No 1T propels a brake-van towards the main-line station.** Neil Sprinks

Left: **Tralee & Dingle 2-6-2T No 5T heads out of Tralee towards the hills of the Dingle Peninsula in August 1993 – despite the fact that the railway closed in 1953. No 5 was built by Hunslet in 1892, emigrated, like so many Kerrymen, to the USA, then, remarkably, came home and was restored to steam to take up work on its native soil once again on the revived 1¼-mile line from Tralee Ballyard, on the edge of the town, to Blennerville.** Author

Above: **No 5T and its two Spanish-built carriages bask in the August sun as they prepare to set off from Blennerville back towards Tralee in August 2004.** Author

Right: **In earlier days, the now preserved No 5T is seen at Annascaul with a cattle special on 29 June 1951.** C. Owen

Below: **The bus service that replaced the trains was an awful lot faster and, in some respects, more comfortable. A CIE Leopard bound for Dingle heads through the hills in August 1974.** Author

FENIT BRANCH

Left: **A mile and a half out of Tralee on the North Kerry line to Limerick, the Fenit branch diverged, although the actual junction was back in Tralee. This is the point of divergence viewed from an AEC railcar working the Tralee to Limerick service on 12 June 1958. Both lines look as if they could do with a visit from the weed-killing train, while one wouldn't fancy anything much heavier than a 'J15' attempting the lightly laid track down to Fenit.** A. E. Bennett

Left: **Opened in 1887, it was hoped that the railway would boost Fenit's chances of becoming a port of some significance, even perhaps attracting transatlantic traffic. This never materialised and the line closed to regular passenger services at the end of 1934. Shortly before that date a 'J15' stands with its train of six-wheelers ready to depart for Tralee.** Author's collection

Below: **Goods traffic continued, and passenger excursions were run on summer Sundays in the 1950s. As can be seen from this view of a diesel railcar set there on 25 June 1959, Fenit's setting is magnificent with the hills and mountains of the Dingle Peninsula across the bay as a backdrop.** D. Thompson

Above: **MGWR 0-6-0T No 560 heads an enthusiasts' tour at Fenit on 5 June 1961.** John Langford

Below: **In the summer of 1974 the track at Fenit was still intact. The line, continuing down on to the pier, had been closed the year before, but beet traffic was worked until the beginning of 1978. Between 1983 and 1988 the Great Southern Railway Preservation Society, based at** Mallow, carried out some refurbishment on the branch, and in its 1985 Year Book wrote 'we have almost completed negotiations for operating the Tralee-Fenit branch as Ireland's first 'preserved' steam railway', but sadly the project eventually folded. Author

NORTH KERRY LINE

Above: **General Motors Bo-Bo No B150 climbs the bank out of Tralee with the daily Limerick goods in August 1969, then swings northwards towards Ardfert and Listowel. The line had closed to passengers in February 1963.** Author

Left: **Ardfert station, August 1969, deep in the north Kerry countryside. Some 4½ miles north of Tralee, it was opened in 1880. Never very busy it was still vital to the rural community it served until road transport gradually eroded its business. It closed to passenger traffic in 1963 but still handled freight until 1978.** Author

Left: **The up and down daily goods trains meet at Listowel in August 1969, each hauled by a re-engined Metro-Vickers A class Co-Co. Despite passenger traffic having ended six years earlier, everything looks neat and tidy and well cared for, with plenty of business on offer for the railway. Listowel was a most important town, an agricultural centre serving North Kerry, as well as being a town with a remarkable literary tradition, its most notable son being John B Keane, an acute observer of everyday life whose work had such appeal that Hollywood took it up. Fergal Keane, the noted BBC correspondent, is his nephew. Before the almost universal ownership of the motor car it would have been unthinkable that Listowel would not have a rail link with the rest of Ireland.** Author

Above: **Another view of the two goods trains in Listowel station, complete with characteristic footbridge. The signalman can be glimpsed through the open door of his box.** Author

Right: **At Listowel station in August 1978, the donkey is standing more or less where the Lartigue monorail used to run.** Author

Below: **At Newcastle West, across the border in County Limerick, Limerick to Tralee trains had to reverse. 'J15' No 175 is running round its train before continuing with the 3.30pm service to Tralee on 29 January 1953.** Neil Sprinks

Above: **Reaching further into 'foreign parts' we arrive at Rathkeale, but permissible I think for the North Kerry ran through a good part of County Limerick, carrying North Kerry people through Abbeyfeale, Newcastle West, Rathkeale and Patrickswell to Limerick city and bringing Limerick city dwellers** to Listowel, where they would board the Lartigue for a seaside excursion. The inevitable 'J15', in this case No 164, is pulling into the station some time in the 1950s. Author's collection

Below: **Still in County Limerick, again the case for the inclusion of this view of** Foynes is powerful for there were several schemes to extend either the standard gauge or the monorail here, on the shores of the River Shannon. No A8R shunts in the goods yard in 1974; passenger services to the station on the left, with its overall roof, had ceased 11 years earlier. Author

LISTOWEL & BALLYBUNION MONORAIL

Right: **A Listowel scene from long ago: the date is actually the mid-1970s, and the farmers are delivering their milk to the creamery. The Volkswagen Beetle and the tractor with the SIN registration are redolent of the period.** Author

Right: **To the outside world Listowel was chiefly famous as the terminus of the remarkable Listowel & Ballybunion monorail. The invention of a French engineer, Henry Lartigue, it opened in 1888 with Leeds-built Hunslet 0-3-0s – now there's a wheel arrangement to savour. Apart from carrying passengers to the small but popular seaside resort of Ballybunion, it did good business bringing back sand for builders' merchants. At holiday times the number of intending passengers, many of them from Tralee and Limerick, stretched its resources beyond what it could cope with, but although its unique double-sided trains, slung each side of the single running rail, were noisy and uncomfortable, it served North Kerry well for 36 years. The Lartigue station at Listowel is seen here with the main-line station alongside.** Kerry Images commercial postcard/National Library of Ireland

Right: **This delightful picture was taken at Listowel shortly before the line shut in 1924. What looks like a family party is standing on one of the step wagons that enabled passengers to cross from one side of the train to the other. The carriage from which the lady in the cloche hat is peering looks rather the worse for wear, not surprising for the railway had been quite badly knocked about during the War of Independence and the subsequent Civil War.** NRM, York

Left: **For some local people, pictures and memories of the Lartigue were not sufficient to keep it alive, and Michael Barry in particular, who farmed at Lisselton, halfway between Listowel and Ballybunion, was assiduous in gathering together all the relics he could come across. By the late 1970s he, seen with cousin Mick (left), had re-erected this length of track in his farmyard.** Author's collection

Above: **Yet even this did not satisfy. If reviving a section of the Tralee & Dingle was remarkable enough, what happened at Listowel in 2003 was the stuff of dreams – nothing short of bringing back the Lartigue! A group of local people got together, money was raised, much of it through the European Community, and in 2003 a section of monorail once again could be ridden upon at its original location in the station yard at Listowel, the train hauled by a diesel-powered replica of an original 0-3-0. Turning the engine: this picture gives a good idea of how the tracks are arranged, the upper one being the running rail and the lower ones being there for guidance.** Author

Left: **The double-sided, back-to-back aspect of the carriages, based on the original designs but built of metal.** Author